MY LUCKY LIFE

IN AND OUT OF
SHOW BUSINESS

DICK VAN DYKE

MY LUCKY LIFE

IN AND OUT OF
SHOW BUSINESS

A MEMOIR

CROWN
ARCHETYPE
NEW YORK

Copyright © 2011 by Point Productions, Inc.

All rights reserved.
Published in the United States by Crown Archetype,
an imprint of the Crown Publishing Group,
a division of Random House, Inc., New York.
www.crownpublishing.com

Crown Archetype with colophon is a trademark of
Random House, Inc.

Library of Congress Cataloging-in-Publication Data
Van Dyke, Dick.
    My lucky life in and out of show business: a memoir /
Dick Van Dyke.
    1. Van Dyke, Dick. 2. Television actors and actresses—
United States—Biography. 3. Comedians—United
States—Biography. I. Title.
PN2287.V335A3   2011
791.45'028'092—dc22
[B]   2010043698

ISBN 978-0-307-59223-1
eISBN 978-0-307-59226-2

Printed in the United States of America

DESIGN BY BARBARA STURMAN
TITLE PAGE PHOTOGRAPH: AP PHOTO/JERRY MOSEY
JACKET DESIGN BY JENNIFER O'CONNOR
JACKET PHOTOGRAPH COURTESY OF THE AUTHOR
Additional photograph credits appear on page 277.

10 9 8 7 6 5 4 3 2 1

First Edition

To my kids

CHRIS, BARRY, STACY, AND CARRIE—

who taught me all I know about love

STAN:
You remember how dumb I used to be?

OLIVER:
Yeah?

STAN:
Well, I'm better now.

—**Laurel and Hardy** (*Block-Heads,* 1938)

If I'm known for giving people decent entertainment
and raising good kids, that's all right.
I'll have lived a good one.

—**Me**

Contents

PART ONE

PART TWO

PART THREE

PART FOUR

FOREWORD

BY CARL REINER

In the last fifty years, I have oft been asked what I consider
to be my most rewarding theatrical experience, and without
hesitation and with total honesty, I say, *"The Dick Van Dyke
Show!"*

Since this is a foreword to Dick Van Dyke's autobiography,
I will not dwell on any of the other talented and brilliant members of that show but on the man whose name inspired its title.
After watching Dick deliver scripted lines that made them seem
cleverer, more elegant, and funnier than I had imagined them to
be, I looked for ways to challenge his ability.

There is one "incident" that Dick did not write about in this
book that I think bears inclusion. It occurred during the rehearsal
of "Gesuntheit, Darling," a second-season episode I'd written during which Rob is afflicted with a sneezing fit. Every time he hugs
or kisses or comes near his son, Ritchie, or his wife, Laura, he

goes into a paroxysm of assorted sneezes that vary in length and volume and comical sounds. Rob, naturally, concludes that he is allergic to his family. As I watched Dick deliver his variety pack of authentic sneezes, I was in awe of his ability to find that many different ways to sneeze while still delivering his lines. Everyone there on the set—the cast and crew and myself—who watched his awesome symphony of sneezes was doubled over with laughter. It was when he finished his performance that I thought, *This man can do anything!*, and to prove it to myself and to the assembly, I asked if he was up to a challenge. Without knowing what I was going to ask, Dick, of course, said yes and I challenged him to do the following:

"Dick, just for fun," I said, "in this order, can you sneeze, cough, belch, hiccup, yawn, and pass gas all while trying to stifle the giggles?"

No sooner were the words out of my mouth than Dick delivered the entire order—and at a rapid-fire pace!

Darn, as I write this, I wonder if he can still do the above and add the "itchy ear," "buzzing bee," and "cinder in his eye" that just popped into my mind.

I'll bet Dick can—and with no apparent effort, for there is no end to that man's kinesthetic abilities. He proved that in 158 episodes of *The Dick Van Dyke Show,* and he continues to do so today.

Viva Van Dyke!

MY LUCKY LIFE

IN AND OUT OF
SHOW BUSINESS

INTRODUCTION

A while ago, but not so long that I can put this story anyplace else and have it make as much sense, my brother, Jerry, had a problem with his kidneys and needed a transplant. While he was on the waiting list, I changed my will to say that he could have mine if I happened to die before he received one. I thought that was pretty considerate, big brotherly, and reflective of the type of person I try to be, and so did he.

In fact, Jerry called me every single day. What a guy, right? Then, as soon as I answered the phone, he said, "Oh, you're still alive."

Yes—and alive I remain. While I have reached that point in life where, like it or not, I am circling the drain, I am happy to report that I am still with all my wits and faculties, still working, still getting calls, and counting my blessings for all of the above.

As such, it seems like a good time to finally jot down some of my life's more important stories, and some of the lesser ones, too.

I have endeavored to write the kind of book I think people want from me. It's also the kind of book that I want from me. It covers my sixty-plus years in show business, including my starring roles in *The Dick Van Dyke Show* and *Mary Poppins*, two projects that have withstood the test of time and will, I am proud to say, likely go on entertaining future generations. I also write about my family, my personal struggles, and a few lessons I may have learned.

As you will discover in the following pages, I never planned any of it. The only career strategy I had was in the early days when my goal was simply to feed my family and keep a roof over their heads. I went where the jobs were, anywhere the wind blew, as I like to say, and most of the time things worked out.

I attribute a lot of it to luck—to being the right person in the right place at the right time.

But a word of warning about this book: If you are looking for dirt, stop reading now. I have had some tough times and battled a few demons, but there is nothing salacious here. I may be a Hollywood anachronism in that way (and possibly in a few other ways). I have tried to write an honest story, with lightness, insight, hope, and some laughs. I have also woven in bits of wisdom, opinion, and lessons learned, like this, my favorite: You can spread jelly on the peanut butter but you can't spread peanut butter on the jelly.

Michelle always liked that one. It made her laugh.

"What does that mean?" she would ask.

"I don't know," I would say. "But it makes a whole lot of sense."

Michelle Triola was my beloved companion of thirty-five years. I always expected her to be looking over my shoulder if and when I wrote this book, reminding me of stories that I might have forgotten. Sadly, she succumbed to cancer shortly after I started this memoir. But in her battle, as in every other aspect of her life, she reminded me of the qualities that go into living a good, full, and meaningful life. Even though she hasn't been here with me, I have still employed her in this effort as my muse, asking many times throughout the process, "Honey, what do you think of this one?"

And it was with her rich, hearty laugh in mind that I decided to start this book with the one true scandal in my life.

PART ONE

---

*Honestly, son, we worried about
you. We didn't think you'd
amount to anything.*

—My father, Loren Van Dyke

✦

1

STEP IN TIME

It was nighttime, February 1943, and I was standing next to my mother, thinking about the war in Europe. I had a very good relationship with my mother, so there's no need for any psychoanalysis about why I was thinking of the war. The fact was, we had finished dinner and she was washing the dishes and I was drying them, as was our routine. My father, a traveling salesman, was on the road, and my younger brother, Jerry, had run off to play.

We lived in Danville, Illinois, which was about as far away from the war as you could get. Danville was a small town in the heartland of America, and it felt very much like the heartland. It was quiet and neighborly, a place where there was a rich side of town and a poor side, but not a bad side. The streets were brick. The homes were built in the early 1900s. Everybody had a backyard; most were small but none had fences.

People left their doors open and their lights on, even when they went out. Occasionally someone down on their luck would knock on the back door and my mother would give him something to eat. Sometimes she would give him an odd job to do, too.

I had things on my mind that night. You could tell from the way I looked out the kitchen window as I did my part of the dishes. I stood six feet one inch and weighed 130 pounds, if that. I was a tall drink of water, as my grandmother said.

"I'm going to be eighteen in March," I said. "That means I'll be up for the draft. I really don't want to go—and I really don't want to be in the infantry. So I'm thinking that I ought to join now and try to get in the Air Force."

My mother let the dish she was washing slide back into the soapy water and dried her hands. She turned to me, a serious look on her face.

"I have something to tell you," she said.

"Yeah?"

"You're already eighteen," she said.

My jaw dropped. I was shocked.

"But how—"

"You were born a little premature," she explained. "You didn't have any fingernails. And there were a few other complications."

"Complications?" I said.

"Don't worry, you're fine now," she said, smiling. "But we just put your birth date forward to what would have been full term."

I wanted to know more than she was willing to reveal, so I turned to another source, my Grandmother Van Dyke. My grandparents on both sides lived nearby, but Grandmother Van Dyke was the most straightforward of the bunch. I stopped by her house one day after school and asked what she remembered about the complications that resulted from my premature birth.

She looked like she wanted to say "bullshit." She asked who had sold me a bill of goods.

"My mother," I replied.

"You weren't premature," she said.

"I wasn't?"

"You were conceived out of wedlock," she said, and then she went on to explain that my mother had gotten pregnant before she and my father married. Though it was never stated, I was probably the reason they got married. Eventually my mother confirmed the story, adding that after finding out, she and my father went to Missouri, where I was born. Then, following a certain amount of time, they returned to Danville.

It may not sound like such a big deal today, but back in 1925 it was the stuff of scandal. And eighteen years later, as I uncovered the facts, it was still pretty shocking to discover that I was a "love child."

I am still surprised the secret was kept from me for such a long time when others knew the truth. Danville was a town of thirty thousand people, and it felt as if most of them were relatives. I had a giant extended family. My great-grandparents on both sides were still alive, and I had first, second, and third cousins nearby. I could walk out of my house in any direction and hit a relative before I got tired.

There were good, industrious, upstanding, and attractive people in our family. There were no horse thieves or embezzlers. I was once given a family tree that showed the Van Dyke side was pretty unspectacular. My great-great-grandfather John Van Dyke went out west via the Donner Pass during the gold rush. After failing to find gold, he resettled in Green County, Pennsylvania.

The same family tree showed that Mother's side of the family, the McCords, could be traced back to Captain John Smith, who established the first English colony in Jamestown, Virginia, in 1607. Maybe it is true, but I never heard any talk about that when I was growing up. Nor have I fact-checked.

The part beyond dispute begins when my father, Loren, or L. W. Van Dyke, met my mother, Hazel McCord. She was a stenographer, and he was a minor-league baseball player: handsome, athletic, charming, the life of the party. And his talent did not end there. During the off-season, he played saxophone and clarinet in a jazz band. Although unable to read a note of music, he could play anything he heard.

He was enjoying the life of a carefree bon vivant until my mother informed him that she was in a family way. All of a sudden the good life as he knew it vanished. He accepted the responsibility, though, marrying my mom and getting a job as a salesman for the Sunshine Cookie Company.

He hated the work, but he always had a shine on his shoes and a smile on his face. Years later, when I saw Arthur Miller's play *Death of a Salesman*, I was depressed for a month. It was my dad's story.

He was saved by his sense of humor. Customers enjoyed his company when he dropped by. Known as Cookie, he was a good time wherever he went. Unfortunately for us, he was usually on the road all week and then spent weekends unwinding on the golf course or hunting with friends. At home, he would have a drink at night and smoke unfiltered Fatima cigarettes while talking to my mother.

He was more reserved around my brother and me, but we knew he loved us. We never questioned it. He was one of those men who did not know how to say the words. A joke was easy. At a party, everyone left talking about what a great guy he was. But a heart-to-heart talk with us boys was not in his repertoire. Years later, after I was married, Jerry and my dad drove to Atlanta to visit us. I asked Jerry what he and Dad had talked about on the drive. He shrugged his shoulders.

"You know Dad," he said. "Not much of anything."

My mother was the opposite. She was funny like my dad, but much more talkative. If she had a deficiency, it was a tendency toward absentmindedness. She once cooked a ham and later found it in my father's shirt drawer. I am not kidding. And when I was in my thirties, she confessed that when I was little she and my father would go to the movies and leave me at home by myself in the crib. I would be a mess when they returned.

"I don't know how I could've done that," she said.

"Me neither," I replied.

"But we were young," she said, smiling. "We didn't mean any harm. We just didn't know any better."

I was five and a half years old when my brother, Jerry, was born. It was not long before my parents moved him from a little bassinet in their room to a crib in my room and made it my job to go upstairs after dinner and gently shake the crib until he went to sleep. Within a year or two, I was given the job of baby-sitting. It wasn't a problem during the daytime when my mom ran errands and was gone a short time, but there were longer stretches at night when my parents went out and our old house filled with strange noises and eerie creaks, and I turned into a wreck.

Convinced that the place was haunted, I would pull a crate into the middle of the house and sit on it with an ax in my lap, ever vigilant and ready to protect my baby brother—and myself!

At six years old, I was sent to kindergarten. There was only one kindergarten in town, and it was located in the well-to-do section. The school was quite hoity-toity. Every morning my mother dressed me up and gave me two nickels. I used one for the six-mile trolley ride to Edison Elementary, and in the afternoon I used my other nickel to get back home.

For first grade, I switched to Franklin Elementary, which was on the other side of town, the side that was struggling even more than we were through the Great Depression. We didn't have much, but the families in this area did not have anything. All the boys at school wore overalls and work shoes—all of them except for me. I arrived on the first day in a Lord Fauntleroy suit, blue with a Peter Pan collar and a beret.

Since I was the only one in class with any schooling, the teacher made me the class monitor and assigned me to escort kids to the bathroom and back. It was a rough job. Some of the kids were crying. Others wanted to go home. I had my hands full all morning. Between my outfit and my job as helper, I was teased for being the teacher's pet.

At recess, I walked outside and a tough kid in overalls— his name was Al—punched me in the chest while another boy kneeled down behind me. Then Al pushed me backward, and I lost my balance and fell down. I ended up with a bloody nose and a few scratches. They also threw my beret on the roof, and for all I know, it is still there.

I was a mess when I got home after school.

"What in God's name happened to you?" my mother said.

I was too much of a little man to rat out the other kids. I spared her the details and simply said, "Mom, I need some overalls."

As for the Depression, I remember my parents having some heated arguments about unpaid bills, and which bills to pay. They went in and out of debt and periodically got a second mortgage on the furniture. I wasn't aware of any hardship and never felt the stigma of having to watch every nickel. Everybody was poor.

Actually, we had it better than most. My maternal grandfather owned a grocery store that also sold kosher meat. He did well. He also owned our house, so we had free rent and food. My other grandfather worked in the shop at the East Illinois Railroad. The train yard was his life. He never took a vacation. If he had time off, he put up storm windows for one of us or fixed a broken door for someone. He was always busy.

On Christmas, we came downstairs in the morning and found him waiting for us, after having lit the tree, started a fire in the fireplace, and gotten everything ready. I looked up to him and, with my father on the road more often than not, he became a role model. He was a seemingly simple, industrious man, but he did a lot of thinking about things, too, and that rubbed off on me.

Thanks to my mother and her mother, there was a good measure of talk about religion in our house when I was growing up. Every summer, I went to Bible school. A bus picked me up across the street from our house early in the morning and brought me back in the afternoon. I hated it. I would rather have played and run around with friends.

Nonetheless, at age eleven, I took it upon myself to read the Bible from front to back. I struggled through the various books, asked questions, and when I reached the end I had no idea what any of it meant. But it pleased my mother and grandmother, who were proud of me and boasted to friends of my accomplishment.

As for my studies in school, I was a solid student. I was strong in English and Latin, but I got lost anytime the subject included math. I wish I had paid more attention to biology and science in general, subjects that came to interest me as an adult. I could have gotten better marks, but I never took a book home, never did homework. Come to think of it, neither of my parents ever looked at any of my report cards. They thought I was a good kid—and looking back, I guess I was.

2

THE YAWN PATROL

J ust before I started ninth grade, my father was transferred to Indiana and we spent a year in Crawfordsville. We took an apartment there. I came into my own. It was not a personality change as much as it was the realization that I *had* a personality. I also found out that I could run and jump pretty well, and I got on the freshman track team. Success on the track added to my self-confidence, including one particular day that still stands out as the most exciting of my life.

We lived across the street from Wabash College, a beautiful little school that gave the town a youthful feel. On Saturdays they hosted collegiate track meets, which our high-school coach helped officiate. I watched all the competitions. This one particular day, Wabash was running against Purdue University and I was in the stands when my coach came up to me and said that the anchorman on the Wabash team had turned his ankle and was unable to run in the race.

"Do you want to run anchor?" he said.

"Are you kidding?" I replied.

"They need a man," he said.

What an offer! I was only fifteen years old, but heck, the chance to compete against college boys was one I did not want to pass up. Even though I didn't have track shoes, which were considered essential to running a good race, since in those days the tracks were layered with cinders, I jumped to my feet. Yes, I told my coach, I was ready to fill in for the Wabash team—and as anchor no less.

When I took the baton, Purdue's anchor was slightly ahead of me. I was not intimidated. We had one hundred yards ahead of us and he did not look that fast to me. I ran hard, gained ground every few steps, and passed him on the outside, with about twenty yards to go.

I heard the crowd roar and held on to the lead, crossing the tape before all the other college boys.

I won.

A high-school freshman.

Amazing.

They gave me a blue ribbon, which I took home and showed my father. He didn't believe me when I said I beat a college boy from Purdue. He thought I was lying. It was, I agreed, pretty far-fetched. The kid I beat was older and could really run. But I was faster—at least that day.

I was voted the most popular boy in the freshman class, but we ended up leaving Crawfordsville and returning to Danville. I envisioned myself starting my sophomore year there as a track star. At my physical, though, the doctor informed me that I had a heart murmur and prohibited me from running, thus ending my high-school athletic career.

I took the news hard, but after a brief funk, I decided the change of course was a sign that I should get serious about my life, and one night at the dinner table I announced that I wanted to become a minister. I knew that would please my mother and her very religious side of the family. The subject also intrigued me intellectually. But pretty soon I lost the fervor that inspired me to carry around a Bible and think deep thoughts. I joined the drama club instead—and found my true calling.

I n those days, plays were written especially for high-school students, and with the war going on, they were mostly all propaganda. I wasn't against being patriotic, but what about a few catchy songs and good jokes? Each one of the musicals, operettas, and comedies we performed was more boring than the one before. I still had fun, but that was really due to discovering the pure enjoyment of being in front of an audience.

I was not alone in that respect. My talented classmates included Donald O'Connor and Bobby Short, both of whom went on to become celebrated performers in their own right, Donald in movies and Bobby as one of the all-time great nightclub entertainers. Bobby could not read a note of music, but he could play anything. He was a human jukebox. We all would entertain one another with songs and make up dance moves.

My closest friends—Bob Walker, Jerry C. Wright, Harold Brown, and Bob Hackman—were also a bunch of talented cutups. We called ourselves the Burfords—Reverend Burford, Grandfather Burford, Cousin Burford, and so on. We got together and harmonized, told jokes, and invented tall tales that kept us amused. We spent hours exercising our imaginations and entertaining ourselves in those days before television and long before the Internet.

Grandfather Burford, aka Bob Hackman, was my best pal. His younger cousin Gene constantly tried to tag along with us and we would let him up to a point. Then Bob would get annoyed and tell him to scram.

Well, Gene grew up and became one of our great actors, winning two Academy Awards and receiving three other nominations. Years later, we ran into each other at a Hollywood event, and as we reminisced about our Danville childhoods, I said that I would have let him hang around if I had known he was going to become a movie star.

B y my junior year, I was a big man on campus. The confidence I had gained as a young athlete affected other areas. I was elected class president and starred in school performances. I had an affable, easy sense of humor that I put to use onstage and in small groups. I enjoyed entertaining people, especially making them laugh, and to that end I cultivated an arsenal of tricks, whether it was a funny face, a pratfall, a joke, or all of the above.

I learned from the best. As a kid, I spent Saturdays in the movie theater. I sat there from eleven in the morning until nine or ten at night, till whenever my mother or father came in and dragged me out. My favorites were the comedians—Charlie Chaplin, Buster Keaton, and Laurel and Hardy. I was particularly taken with Stan Laurel.

From an early age, Stan was my idol. I delighted my parents and friends endlessly with my impersonations of him. I turned into Stan at any and every occasion. No one paid much attention, though. As I explained years later at Stan's funeral, that was because every other kid in the neighborhood was doing his own impression of Stan Laurel.

I also loved to sing, though I was not among the singing teacher's favorites. I tried out for the school's a cappella group every time there was an audition, and every time the teacher turned me down. She only let me in, finally, when they ran out of basses.

School was a playground for me. In and out of the classroom, I had a great time. It did my poor brother no good. As he came along, all he heard was "Your brother Dick did this" and "Dick did that," and it pissed him off. He became well-known as a trouble-maker. After I graduated, he was called to the dean's office one day for some infraction, and instead of listening to a long repri-mand he hit the dean in the jaw and knocked him down. Need-less to say, that stunt got Jerry kicked out of school, and he had to drive twenty miles every day to the next closest high school in order to get his diploma.

S hortly before my seventeenth birthday, I spotted an ad in the local newspaper for a job as a part-time announcer at the local CBS radio outlet, WDAN. I had been searching for jobs. Friends of mine working at the market were making eleven bucks a week. The radio station, which had lost a few announcers to the draft, was paying only eight dollars a week. But it was radio, so who cared?

I auditioned and got the job. I worked after school and on weekends, from ten P.M. to midnight. I referred to my show as *The Yawn Patrol,* but that was hardly true. It was a dream job. In this little station, I did everything: I played records, read the news, gave the weather report, wrote my own commercials, and even sold my own advertising. If a breaking story came in from New York, I patched it in myself.

Even if nothing big happened, each night was a thrilling adventure, an experience that made life seem large and important. I felt like I was at the center of the world, and in a town as small as Danville, I was. People tuned in for information, and I was the one giving it to them. I almost lost the job a few times, though. There were several Saturday nights when friends of mine came down to the station and danced in the lobby, and we got caught having a party. That was a no-no.

But it was hard to resist such temptation. As jobs went, I had the coolest one in town, especially among my age group. I tried to look the part by getting myself a pair of thick horn-rimmed glasses like Dave Garroway, a popular radio personality long before he became the first host of NBC's *Today* show. Through Dave and other shows like his, I discovered Sarah Vaughan, jazz, and the pop music of the day.

Every once in a while I tried to air some of the hotter stuff I liked, such as Stan Kenton or a short-lived group called Sauter Finnegan that played chords like nobody was playing in those days. But whenever I snuck something progressive into the playlist, I was called on the carpet. My bosses wanted Glenn Miller and nothing too far to the left or right of him.

Occasionally I made a mistake. I had these sixteen-inch disks with a number of cuts on them that provided an intro to the news, or in the case of the weather, a bouncy little ditty that went, "Oh Mister Weatherman, what's the weather today . . ." Then I came in and read the forecast. Well, one night I put on the wrong cut, and without immediately realizing it I played a tornado warning.

It sounded like an emergency broadcast. *Attention, attention, everyone. A tornado is heading for the city. Stay near your homes, make sure you're near shelter, and stay tuned to this station.*

Once I heard what had happened, I tried, without sounding alarmed, to correct it. There was no tornado! There was no storm! But it was too late. Every single one of the station's phone lines lit up. The switchboard looked like a Fourth of July fireworks display. Blinking lights everywhere. People wanted to know where the storm was coming from, when it was going to hit, and how strong it was.

Fortunately, I managed to straighten things out over the air before anyone panicked or complained. Thankfully, I didn't get fired. But I didn't last much longer, either.

In March 1942, I signed up for the Air Force. The thought of getting drafted, put in the infantry, and charging through the front lines filled me with dread. "Anything but that," I told myself. And anyone else who asked why I had signed up when they found out it meant I would not finish high school and get my diploma.

But there was a glitch. I went to the nearest Air Force base and spent all day taking IQ and psychological tests. I returned the next day for my physical, which I passed. No heart murmur whatsoever. Not even a whisper. I was in great shape, with one exception. I didn't weigh enough.

I was too skinny! I tipped the scale at 135 pounds, and at my height I had to weigh 141.

I took the test three times and didn't make it. I weighed even less the second and third times from sweating nervously at the thought of being sent to the front lines. I had one more chance. I went to Chicago and stayed in a motel overnight. In the morning before my weigh-in I ate half a dozen bananas, and then just before I got on the scale I darted into the men's room and drank as much water as I could.

I barely made it, but that was all that mattered. I was in.

I did my basic training in Wichita Falls, Texas, and then entered pilot's training in Toledo, Ohio. I envisioned myself as a fighter pilot, which did not make sense given my severe allergy to combat. It turned out to be a moot point. The closest I got to my pilot's wings was when the other trainees and I serviced the planes.

Most of the work I did was classwork. I took physics, math, and aeronautics at the College Training Detachment. I enjoyed learning and did well. But I failed every military-related exam I took. The captain called me into his office one day and showed me the tests arrayed on his desk.

"They are all failing grades," he said. "You tested out with an IQ of a hundred and fifty. I don't get it."

"Sir, I'm not much of a soldier," I said.

But I looked good in the uniform. I was one of about fifty military guys in town, and so the girls were all over the place. Finally our commanding officer called all of us in one day, had us stand at attention in the classroom, and informed us that the Air Force was about to join in a major push against Japan.

"Some of you will be sent overseas as tail gunners," he said. "Others of you will be assigned according to your abilities."

I started singing and dancing right there and was subsequently assigned to special services.

3

SPECIAL SERVICES

Getting into special services was the best thing that could have happened to me—and the Air Force.

I was assigned to special services after being stationed at Majors Field in Sherman, Texas. We built and painted sets, put on plays, and starred in sketch-filled variety shows. That was about as military as I wanted to get, and as luck would have it, not much more was required. Our CO was a woman, a former Broadway star in the 1930s. We had her wrapped around our little finger. We were able to wrangle a three-day pass anytime we wanted. I even got out of KP after talking someone in the mess hall into letting me build a little booth in the corner where I played records and read the news.

The highlight of my Air Force career came one day as I left a meeting and spotted a notice on the bulletin board saying the base's radio station was looking for an announcer for its daily entertainment show, *Flight Time*. I signed up immediately. A few days later, I was standing at the latrine when a guy came in and asked if I was Van Dyke.

"Yeah," I said.

His name was Byron Paul. After getting himself situated at the latrine next to me, he handed me a piece of paper and said, "Read it." It turned out to be my audition. I got the job right there—and in Byron, I made a new friend who would eventually become a cameraman at CBS, rise to the position of director, and play an integral role in bringing me to that network.

As the host of *Flight Time,* I played music, read the news, and delivered the wartime information the Air Force wanted disseminated to their men. It was done from a tiny station in town, which meant I left the base daily and felt as if I was coasting through the war in a role that was perfect for me.

I was also great at close-order drills. That was like dancing. The faster they did it, the better I liked it. I was light, quick, and agile. I was always the first one through the obstacle course, too. But if something didn't involve speed or agility, I was sunk. Every Wednesday, for instance, the cadets had to run five miles. I finished last every time. I didn't have any stamina.

Nor did I have the kind of discipline needed for the military. There were little signs, like the fact that my clothes were never clean. Early in the morning, I could frequently be seen running outside in my Air Force–issue boxers, stealing other guys' uniform shirts off the laundry line because mine were always dirty. But there were bigger issues, too, indicating that I wasn't cut out for the Air Force.

One day I hitched a ride back home with a captain who was flying to Rantoul, Illinois, about thirty miles from Danville. I don't know why he invited me to tag along, but I was in as soon as he said he could get me a three-day pass. I conveniently forgot to mention to him that despite being in the Air Force and in pilot training, I had never been off the ground in a plane.

As we took off in his twin-engine UC-78, he began complaining that he had a bad hangover, and then once we were in the air, he said he wanted to get some sleep. He showed me the altimeter, gave me the direction on the compass, and told me to keep the plane at a certain altitude. Within minutes, he was snoring—and I was screaming like an old lady. I was petrified. Every gust of wind blew the plane this way or that, causing me to grip the controls even tighter. I had no idea what to do. I thought I was going to die.

I flew straight over Illinois. We were midway across Indiana when the captain finally woke up.

"How you doing?" he asked.

"Sir, I have to be honest," I said. "This is the worst experience of my life. I don't know if I ever want to fly again."

After the war, I returned home and got my old job back at the radio station. It was 1945, and I was nearly twenty years old. I had to start to put my life together. I began dating Margie Willet, a local girl I had known for years. All through high school, she had dated a boy who was on both the football and wrestling teams. His neck was thicker than my entire body. After she ditched him for me, he wanted to kill me. We would be sitting in her parents' living room and suddenly hear him out front, yelling, "Van Dyke, come out here! I'll bust you up." Given that he loved to fight, I took that as my signal to race out the back door. He never did catch on—or catch me.

With a girlfriend, I got more serious about my life and went into the advertising business with Wayne Williams, the son of a prominent physician in town. Wayne was older than I was, elegant, well-educated, and ambitious. We opened an office, hired a secretary, and sold advertising for an hour-long radio show that I did five days a week. The show featured one of my earliest characters, an old man named Bartholomew Cuzy, who did man-on-the-street bits.

In my free time, I joined an amateur theater group in town, the Red Mask Players, and starred in a number of plays, including *No Time for Comedy*. I was swimming along pretty comfortably until shortly after my twenty-first birthday, when Wayne moved to Chicago to work for another, bigger advertising company.

I understood. We were running our business in a small town and there was very little margin. Although profitable, the business wasn't going to grow much beyond where we'd already taken it. We couldn't simply add 15 percent to costs as companies in New York and Chicago did.

I returned to the radio station full-time. I just didn't have the head for business. Without Wayne, I knew that I would starve. I enjoyed being on the radio, not selling.

But I had a sense that television was coming on strong, that it was going to be the next big thing, and I thought I could do well as an announcer. It wasn't that different from what I was already doing. I heard about an opening at WBBM in Chicago and arranged for an audition. I took a train there the night before and stayed in a cheap hotel. My wakeup call never came and I slept through my appointment.

Upset, I went to the station, anyway. I knew I wasn't going to get anywhere without at least trying. Dave Garroway worked at WBBM, and I wondered if I'd catch a glimpse of him. As it turned out, I did. At the station, I wandered into the announcers' lounge and there he was, the great man in his horn-rimmed glasses. He turned to me and said, "Kid, this is private." I knew that he meant *Get lost.* I didn't even have a chance to say hello.

I later auditioned at an ABC station in Indianapolis. They turned me away, too, saying my voice didn't sound folksy enough. Getting into TV was not as easy as I thought.

It was about then, the summer of 1947, that I crossed paths with Phil Erickson. Though our families were friendly, Phil was four years older than I was, old enough that I didn't know him in high school. But I knew of him. He had been active in dramatics and then developed an act called the Three Make-Believes. They lip-synced to songs and turned into a novelty that did quite well across the country.

But they'd recently broken up following a booking in Chicago. One of his partners decided to go to law school and the other guy made plans, too. So Phil returned to Danville and came into the theater one afternoon looking for a new partner. I was rehearsing *The Philadelphia Story.* He introduced himself and asked, "Do you want to do an act with me? I have a booking in California."

I wanted out of there so badly that I didn't bother asking about specifics. I just said, "What time will you pick me up?"

4

THE MERRY MUTES

The funny thing was that Phil never auditioned me. He never asked, "Can you lip-sync to a record? Can you perform?"

He just pulled up in front of my house one day in a beat-up Chevy, I hopped in, and we drove west. Phil was married, with two babies, and had left his family in Danville. He fell asleep a few times on the drive and I quickly had to grab the wheel to keep us in our lane. Even today I can still hear myself yelling, in an alarmed voice, "Phil! Phil! Wake up!"

We stayed in a couple of cheap motels along the way, and when we got to California, we pooled together what little money we had to rent a little tract home in Venice. It was a dull-colored cracker box without any landscaping—no trees, no shrubs, and brown patches of weeds where there once might have been a green lawn.

I didn't care. Phil had taken a risk by asking me to partner up, and even though for me it was more of a lark and an adventure, I felt a responsibility to him and an obligation to our partnership as the Merry Mutes. The prospect of getting up in front of a paying audience also filled me with a mix of fear and excitement that would prove to be a lifelong addiction.

Would they like us?

Could I make them laugh and have a good time?

We would see.

We were booked into the Zephyr Room at the Chapman Park Hotel, an old, odd place that was all tiny cottages spread across a block near the Brown Derby restaurant and across the street from L.A.'s landmark hotel, the Ambassador, which was home to the famous Coconut Grove. The Zephyr was quite a bit smaller, to say the least.

On opening night, Phil and I arrived early and checked out the stage. We were well-rehearsed by this point, yet we still went over our act again before anyone was there. I was beyond nervous. My skin was pale and my knees knocked like shutters in a windstorm. After I threw up my dinner, I am sure Phil wondered what he had gotten himself into.

But he was understanding and patient. He gave me space to be sick, then talked me through my jitters, assuring me in a soft, steady, confident voice that we were going to be fine, and then, before I had a chance to think, I was staring into a spotlight.

Our act was deceptively simple. We satirized the popular songs and singers of the day, like Bing Crosby, Mary Martin, and Spike Jones and the City Slickers. If a song was hot, we worked it into the act. The opening night audience at the Zephyr loved us, and so did audiences on subsequent nights. We were a hit. We were booked there for weeks, long enough that Phil moved his family to L.A.

Margie was still back in Danville. She regularly asked when I was going to send for her. We were engaged, so her hints became less subtle as time passed. I did not blame her. But I knew sending for her meant we would get married, and to be frank, I couldn't afford it.

Phil and I were making $150 a week and he took a little more than a fifty-fifty split since he had a family. Even with all of us sharing a house, we were still barely getting by. I did not know what to do.

On the one hand, I wanted to settle down and get married one day. On the other hand, I worried whether I could afford that day anytime soon.

I was in a spot.

The solution presented itself in a most convenient fashion one day after Phil and I got to work. It was early, well before showtime, and I was wandering around the hotel when I began talking to this wonderful guy who produced a radio show called *Bride and Groom*. Broadcast from the hotel's chapel, each show told the story of a couple's courtship and then culminated with their wedding. As a gift, the couple received a free honeymoon.

I mentioned that I wanted to get married but couldn't afford it, and the producer, who dropped in on our act all the time, invited me to get married on his show. They would pick up the whole tab, plus send us on a honeymoon.

It sounded like a deal to me. Margie was all for it, too.

Borrowing money, I sent her a one-way train ticket, and on February 12, 1948, we exchanged "I do"s in front of a minister and two radio microphones as an estimated 15 million people listened in. For our honeymoon, the show sent us on a ten-day skiing vacation to Mount Hood, in Oregon. I had never skied before, but we had a wonderful time. The best part was that it didn't cost us a nickel. Which was perfect, since we didn't have a nickel to spare. Back in L.A., Margie and I lived with Phil and his wife and their two kids. We had one small bedroom to ourselves, no car, and if we wanted to do something, we had to walk or hop on the trolley.

After a while, we finally rented our own apartment in Laurel Canyon. It was actually a guesthouse behind someone else's home on Lookout Mountain Road. We had a room and a kitchenette—and privacy.

L.A. was gorgeous back then. There were no high-rise buildings, and the words *traffic* and *smog* were unheard of. In the morning, the canyon filled with fog that gradually gave way, as the sun rose, to breathtaking views, almost as if a curtain were being lifted on the day. Depending on the time of the year, the air was ripe with the fragrance of orange blossoms, honeysuckle, and other flowers, and the mostly undeveloped hills were still home to deer and other wildlife that made it seem as if you were far from the city.

One day I came home and Margie rushed out to meet me. She was as surprised as I'd ever seen her, and for good reason. She had been startled out of the house by a strange noise—our new car. I had driven home in a 1935 Ford Phaeton convertible that I'd bought for $125. After inspecting our new car, she gave me a puzzled look.

"Where is it?" she asked.

"What?" I said.

"The top."

"That's why I was able to afford it," I said.

"What do you mean?" she asked.

"It doesn't have a top," I explained. "It's long gone."

It didn't have a second gear, either. It only had first and third, making it difficult to get up the steep hill to our house. Getting down was only slightly easier. Every morning the battery was dead and I had to coast down the hill to the gas station to get a jump. And when it rained, which fortunately was not often in L.A., I got drenched. But I drove that thing for a long time.

A while after our Zephyr Room debut, Phil and I were booked into Slapsy Maxie's, one of Hollywood's hottest clubs, as the opening act for the Delta Rhythm Boys. We signed for two shows a night. It was our biggest gig to date. On opening night, I looked out and saw Lucille Ball in the audience. She was not laughing. Nor was anyone else. We died. We weren't sophisticated enough for a club drawing from Hollywood's upper tier, and nobody applauded when we finished. Oh, it was painful.

Afterward two guys knocked on our dressing-room door, gave us thirty bucks, and told us to get out. We never even made the late show. Adding insult to injury, I went outside and found my car had been towed. I eventually found it in a muddy field, buried up to the hubcaps, and spent the rest of the night trying to get it out. It was one of those moments when you ask, "Jeez, am I in the wrong business?"

Word of that debacle spread through the nightclub world and we lost a number of bookings. During that fallow period, Phil bought a TV, one of the seven-inch sets that were on the market. We watched Milton Berle's *Texaco Star Theater, The Ed Sullivan Show, Candid Camera, Ted Mack's Amateur Hour,* and the news. Our dry spell was broken when a local station booked our act.

One of the few TV stations in L.A. at the time, it broadcast from the top of Mount Wilson, about ninety minutes northeast of L.A.

Phil and I drove there in my '35 Ford. We got about halfway up the mountain, one of the tallest peaks in Southern California, when the car died. It didn't just wheeze and cough. It literally passed out. We took our junk out and hiked the rest of the way up.

Less than a year later, Margie and I found a duplex in Malibu. We moved in and for about eight months loved living at the beach. We found out she was pregnant with twins while Phil and I were working at the Georgian Hotel in Santa Monica, which was much closer to where I lived than Hollywood, and I carved out an easy routine with the shorter drive.

A problem arose when my share of the Merry Mutes's take failed to cover all of Margie's and my expenses. I fell behind on the rent, and though I always felt like something would happen that would allow me to catch up, our bills piled up until I had what was easily the worst day of my life.

It started one day with Margie experiencing severe cramps. When she began to bleed, I drove her to St. John's Hospital in Santa Monica. I am sure our old Ford had never been pressed to go as fast as I implored it on that gray afternoon. I had gone to church and Sunday school every week through childhood, right up until I joined the Air Force, and there in the car I said every prayer I had ever learned.

Half of those prayers were for Margie, and the other half were for our car. "Please, God, get her through this." It didn't matter if God understood which was which; I covered all bases.

Shortly after we got to the hospital, Margie miscarried, and it was a very bleak time for us. You figure things happen for a reason, and that was one of those times. I left her resting at the hospital and returned home to find all of our belongings stacked up in front of our place, on the shoulder of the highway. Our landlord had thrown us out.

He was apologetic, more so than might be expected from someone who was owed three months' rent. But he was also being practical. As he explained, he needed the money.

Well, I didn't have it. I turned around and, with cars speeding past, began piling our belongings in the back of our Ford.

I went back to St. John's and spent the night with Margie. In the morning, I used most of the last eighty-five dollars I had to my name to pay the hospital bill. With the meager amount left over, we got a room with a hot plate in a shack of a hotel on Sawtelle Boulevard. Margie was lactating, bandaged, sore, and tired. I bought cheap hamburger meat and cooked it on that small griddle. It was a pretty bad moment in our lives.

A few nights later, I stared at the ceiling while Margie slept. I didn't know if we could make it. I wondered if we should go back to Danville, where we had family to help us through tough times.

"Guess what?"

It was Phil, calling a week or so later with good news. We met at a nearby coffee shop and over breakfast he broke the good news. We had a job in San Diego. Not only did we have work, but the club was putting us up as well. We had free lodging. Hallelujah, I thought. My prayers had been answered.

Margie and I were so broke, though, that my father-in-law, who worked at a Chevrolet dealership outside of Chicago, brought a 1941 Chevy to L.A. and handed me the keys so we would be able to get to San Diego. I can't imagine how events might have played out if we hadn't been able to get there.

Our weeklong gig at Tops was a big, much-needed success. It turned into a total of four weeks, long enough for Margie and me to regroup, and then we headed to another job, a club in Pocatello, Idaho.

In penny-pinching mode, I thought I could make the 1,200-mile trip, without stopping, in one twenty-four-hour swoop. I was wrong—a fact I was made aware of somewhere outside of Salt Lake City when Margie punched my arm and screamed at me to "wake up!"

I was asleep with my eyes open and headed into oncoming traffic.

"Oh Jesus, I'm on the wrong side of the road!" I shouted as I swerved back onto the right side.

"Yeah, because you were asleep!" she said, alarmed and angry that I had stubbornly insisted on driving straight through.

In Pocatello, we met up with Phil, and the two of us performed on the same bill with the folksinger Burl Ives. At the end of the week, the club owner skipped town and we never got paid. While we were driving back to L.A., the timing gear blew and our car broke down in the mountains outside of Reno. It was about one A.M., cold, and we were in the middle of nowhere. We got out to look around and heard coyotes howling. I thought we were done.

After a while, a big old truck came along and stopped. The driver got out a long, thick chain, tied our car to the back of his truck, and pulled us down the hill. When we hit the curves, we were whipped to the very edge and several times thought we were going over the cliff. We made it to Reno, though, and checked into a hotel after dropping the car off at a mechanic.

Then we had another problem. I had no idea how we were going to pay for the car repairs or our hotel. We were broke.

I stepped into a phone booth outside the hotel and called my father and father-in-law, hoping one of them could wire us money. But neither had any extra funds. I slid the phone booth door open and lit a cigarette, wondering what I was going to do.

As soon as I walked into the hotel room, Margie saw the worried expression on my face. I told her the facts. We had thirty dollars—that was it. I put the cash on the dressing table and took off my coat and collapsed on the bed. I had been driving all the way from Pocatello, then fretting about our fate. I could barely keep my eyes open.

The next thing I knew, I heard Margie coming back into the room. She turned on the lights and I saw that her eyes were as wide as saucers.

"You aren't going to believe it," she said.

"What?" I asked.

She opened her hands and showed me a fistful of money.

"I took the thirty dollars to the blackjack table," she said, "and won!"

It was not a lot of money. But it paid for the hotel, got the car fixed, and allowed us to get home.

After we regrouped, Phil and I went back on the road, starting at the Chi Chi Club in Palm Springs. We were onstage, pantomiming to the Bing Crosby–Mary Martin hit "Wait Till the Sun Shines, Nellie," when an earthquake struck and shook the ground beneath us, as well as the walls and ceiling, the tables and glasses, and everything else in the club, including our record. It skipped from one song to another. Rather than stop, Phil and I tried to keep up—changing lyrics every couple seconds and exchanging panicked looks—and the audience roared.

Afterward, we hurried offstage, confused, dripping in flop sweat, and wondering what the hell had just happened. The club's manager, a grin plastered across his narrow face, rushed over and threw his arms around us.

"I loved the earthquake bit," he exclaimed. "Keep it in the act."

Phil looked at me over the manager's shoulder.

"It was an earthquake," he mouthed.

"Oh my God," I replied without making a sound. "Let's not keep it in the act."

We continued to shake things up, though, at the Last Frontier in Las Vegas and the Golden Hotel in Reno, where I met the young piano sensation of the time, Liberace. He was packing them in down the street, but one night he caught a bit of our act and told me that he thought I had some talent. You wouldn't have known that from our reception at New York's Blue Angel. The weekend tourists lapped up our act, but the more sophisticated Manhattanites who showed up during the week thought we were rubes—and we were fired.

Miami turned out to be our place. We headlined Martha Raye's Five O'Clock Club for an entire season—all winter. I brought Margie, who felt like she was on a long vacation. It was a good time, one that got even better, almost too good to be true. One day, after leaving Margie in our room, I was on my way to meet Phil to discuss adding some new bits to the act when one of the men who ran the club directed me into his office.

He couldn't have been friendlier as he closed the door and explained that Phil and I were doing an excellent job, but he especially liked me. He said that he was impressed with my singing, dancing, and all-around ability to entertain. He and his partner, he added, had noticed the way the audience related to me and they had a proposition for me.

"As you can tell, we think you have special talent," he said. "Basically, we'd like to take you over."

"You want to take over Phil's and my act?" I asked.

"No, just you," he said. "We're looking at you as a single."

"Well, thank you for the compliment," I said, "but I still don't understand the, um, proposal."

He explained that he and his partner ran the club with a group of "silent investors," men who, he said, preferred to stay in the background but who trusted their judgment of talent. He said they liked the way the audiences reacted to me and wanted to invest in my act.

"But I don't have an act," I said.

"We'll help you build it," he said, adding that they would get behind me in every way, from writing to PR to salary.

"Really?" I said.

"We'll pay you fifteen thousand a week," he said.

At the time, Phil and I were splitting less than 5 percent of that, or about seven hundred dollars a week. My eyes glazed over.

"It's a good starting salary," he continued. "We'll have the act written. You'll buy your wardrobe. And we'll take care of all your bookings."

Deep down I knew I was not going to leave my partner in the lurch, but the sum of money being offered was so fantastic that it was impossible to simply dismiss it. In truth, I was blown away. I did not know how to respond. Nor did I seem able to. My mouth seemed temporarily out of order. Finally I stammered a thank-you and explained that I would talk about it with my wife and agent and get back to him as soon as possible.

"You're never going to believe what happened," I told Margie.

Like me, she was speechless.

"How much money are they going to pay you?" she asked.

I returned to Earth after speaking to Phil's and my Atlanta-based agent, Monk Arnold. He had me repeat the details, then woke me up from this dream of having arrived on easy street.

"Dick, they're the Mob," he said.

"You think?" I asked.

"Dick, if they get a hold of you like this, they've got you for the rest of your life."

I shut my eyes and took a deep breath, feeling a wave of disappointment pass through me.

"Don't fool with them," Monk advised.

"It did sound too good," I said.

"If it sounds too good to be true, it probably is," he said.

I had Monk Arnold call the guy back and tell him that I had too many commitments and would not feel right changing course. But I implored him to convey how flattered I was at the same time. I wanted to stay on good terms with those guys. I did not want them mad at me.

5

LIVE ON THE AIR

I n 1949, Phil and I got a job in Atlanta at the Henry Grady Hotel, an excellent establishment with a large ballroom. We performed two shows a day, one in the afternoon for kids and another at night for a more mature crowd. Children's favorites and slapstick were de rigueur for the early show, and then we spiced up the nighttime routine with Spike Jones, Bing Crosby, and popular songs on the radio, as well as more mature jokes.

With Phil as the straight man, more or less, and me in the role of rubber-limbed comedian, tirelessly mugging, miming, dancing, and inventing antics on the spot, we filled the room every show. We also did local events, radio, and even store openings. All the exposure made us quite popular around town. In turn, Phil and I fell in love with the city.

At the time, Atlanta still felt like a small city. With only about 250,000 people living there, it was quaint, comfortable, and affordable. Charmed by the surroundings and buoyed by our success, both of us decided to put stakes in the ground. We took advantage of the GI Bill and bought homes. Mine was a tiny three-bedroom with prefabricated sides that seemed to go up in days. Even as the workmen slapped it together, Margie and I beamed with the pride of new and naive homeowners.

The backyard was up against the woods, and though we had only a couple flower beds, shrubs, and several baby trees, it looked to me, with my vivid imagination, like the grounds of an estate. Wanting the front to look good, too, I carted in umpteen wheelbarrows of sod and had it looking like a magazine ad—until a hard rain washed all that greenery and hard work away.

In 1950, Margie gave birth to our son Chris, and thirteen months later we had a second baby boy, Barry. Like Phil, now that I had a family, I lost my taste for the road. I got a job as an announcer at the local CBS radio station, WAGA. Pretty soon they gave me my own slot as an early-morning disk jockey, and a little later, when there was an opening at night for a fifteen-minute record act, Phil and I took it.

You couldn't be in Atlanta for any appreciable amount of time without hearing me, which worked in my favor when the local television station owned by the *Atlanta Constitution,* WCON, needed a full-time announcer. They turned to me. I got the job reading all the news, announcements, and commercials—anything that needed announcing over the course of an eight-hour day.

I proved myself adept and inexpensive, and eventually the station's management gave me an hour-long show of my own. I was thrilled.

But let me tell you, no matter how excited and eager I was to do well—and I was—it didn't take long before those sixty minutes felt like six hundred minutes. It ate up material. I mean it devoured material. Few things are as terrifying as standing in front of a camera by yourself and realizing you have used most of your best material and still have to fill fifty-four minutes.

On my first night, I felt like the clock had stopped. It didn't seem like the hour would ever end. I read the newspaper, told jokes, and interviewed people—whatever I could think of. It was like an episode of *The Twilight Zone*. A young performer's dream comes true when he's given his own hour-long television show, except when that hour never ends and the performer goes bananas.

Fortunately, I figured out the pacing and quickly got to where I was so comfortable in front of the camera that I forgot I was on the air. I never gave it a thought—until the red light on the camera went off and I began to think about the next day's material.

I never worked as hard. At night, I sat in front of the TV with Margie and the boys, with a portable typewriter on my lap, and read through the newspaper, through joke books, and listened to the TV, all the while writing furiously.

Was it quality material?

I had no idea. But I got very good at producing a lot of it.

I pantomimed records, told jokes, and interviewed people on the street about popular topics. I also came up with a running bit where I put some soft clay on a slant board and told a story while I sculpted. I kept the bit going throughout the hour. At the end of one show, I put the finishing touches on a guy and then punched him under the chin. His face scrunched up and I quipped, "Well, there's a funny-looking old fart."

This was the early 1950s, when there were only a few stations on the dial, and oh my God, the phone calls poured into the station. I was almost fired.

Eventually the station moved into a more proper studio and I partnered with a quick-witted woman named Fran Adams (later

Fran Kearton) on *The Fran and Dick Show,* also known as *The Music Shop.* We wrote and produced skits, clowned around, satirized popular TV shows, and pantomimed hit songs. Like all such shows done live, it was a little bit of everything we could think of.

In her 1993 memoir, Fran recalled a play on the show *Dragnet,* with Detective Friday and his partner, Thursday, investigating the murder of Goldilocks, of "Goldilocks and the Three Bears" fame. She was found on the street "wearing a derby and slacks," intoned Friday. "At least she died like a man," said Thursday. Ugh. As I said, it was everything we could think of.

One day, as I was lip-syncing Andy Griffith's 1953 comedy hit "What It Was, Was Football," a monologue about a hillbilly preacher watching his first football game and trying to figure out what was happening on "the pretty little green cow pasture," I looked up and saw Andy himself, watching me.

It turned out he was in town promoting his record, but no one told me he was stopping by the studio. I was too far into the bit to stop. I thought, Oh, God, I'm in trouble. He's not going to appreciate my interpretation. (Given the quality of the *Dragnet* satire, you can only imagine.)

But Andy was quite amused.

And I was quite relieved.

At some point, I left Fran and repartnered with Phil on a show for WSP, the local NBC affiliate. The show was more elaborate than anything either of us had done up to that point. We had a little band, a girl singer, and a kid who helped us write. In other words, it was a real show.

We embraced the challenge of producing what was essentially a variety show every day. We poured every ounce of creative energy into writing sketches and rehearsing songs. I even painted scenery on the weekends. I was so passionate that I was nearly possessed. It was also fun, and the show was quite popular—or so we thought. We figured we would do it a long time.

Phil had also opened a comedy club called The Wit's End. It was located near the Biltmore Hotel and Georgia Tech University. The club's motto was to the point: "Bring money." And people did. It was an instant hit with the college kids and would, by the 1970s, send improv groups all over the country. In its early days, though, it complemented our TV show.

After about a year, the TV station's general manager came to me and said they wanted me to do the show alone.

"What about Phil?"I asked.

The station manager shook his head.

I raised my eyebrows. I didn't know what that meant.

"We want you to do it," he said. "We don't need Phil."

I felt a pit in my stomach. I had been in this situation before. Now, granted, it wasn't the Mob making me an offer. It was the station manager. But he was persuasive. He said they were going to cut back and fire Phil, anyway. They didn't want to pay two people for a job they thought one person could do adequately enough.

I needed a job, but I couldn't leave Phil hanging like that. I didn't know what to do until I remembered that some months earlier a New Orleans TV station had contacted me about a job. I ignored them at the time, but I found out the position was still available, and though it paid the same as I currently made, two hundred dollars a week, I took it. It still meant breaking up with Phil, but I thought it was better than continuing to do *our* show without him.

I didn't tell him about my conversation with the station

manager, and he was hurt when I left. He thought I was deserting him. Later, we talked it out and patched things up, and moved on with our lives and careers.

It was 1954 when we arrived in the Big Easy, and on my first day in town, before I had even visited the station, I met the general manager at a motel. He took me into a conference room, where I improvised for about a half hour in front of a half dozen potential sponsors. They were local businessmen and regional reps for larger companies. They wanted to see what I had to offer.

Talk about pressure. And poor conditions for a performance. But I knew my livelihood was on the line. If I didn't get sponsors, they would find someone else and I would have to look for work.

Luckily, I nabbed a couple of them, including a biggie, Louisiane Coffee. My new boss gave me a congratulatory slap on the back and then I went back to my motel, downed two beers, and passed out.

Once past that stressful day, New Orleans felt charmed. Margie and I had a cute little house and pretty soon we added our third child and first daughter, Stacy. The station was located in the French Quarter, and I was able to walk to work in the morning as the restaurateurs and barkeeps cleaned up from the previous night and cafés brewed fresh coffee. It was nice.

For the show, I had a combo of musicians, did some man-on-the-street interviews, and brought kids into the studio, which was almost always comedy gold. I incorporated them into skits and songs. I had learned a lot over the years and was very comfortable in front of the camera. Within about six months, I owned the New Orleans market. I was beating Arthur Godfrey's national broadcast, which, in those days, was something.

My ratings got the attention of the network in New York, specifically my old Air Force buddy Byron Paul. We had kept in touch over the years as Byron rose up the ranks at CBS, from a cameraman to a director. He told the executives about me and suggested they bring me to New York for an audition.

There was some skepticism, of course, but Byron said if they didn't hire me, he would personally pay all of the expenses. I heard that and said, "Really? That's very generous—and brave—of you." But he felt confident it was not going to cost him a cent.

6

A SEVEN-YEAR
CONTRACT

Jane Froman was a popular singer from the 1930s, a former star with the Ziegfeld Follies, and so highly regarded that legendary Broadway producer Billy Rose reportedly once quipped that the ten best female singers in the world were "Jane Froman and nine others." In 1943 she survived a plane crash in Europe while on a USO tour but suffered injuries that led to a rash of physical problems as well as an addiction to painkillers and alcohol.

In 1952, the same year Susan Hayward played her in the movie *With a Song in My Heart,* Jane began hosting a nightly fifteen-minute show on CBS called *USA Canteen.* By the time I arrived in New York City for my audition, her show was called simply *The Jane Froman Show.* On the night I got into town,

Byron met me at my hotel and took me to the theater where she did her show.

I was backstage with Byron when Jane finished her show, and I heard the director ask the audience to stay in their seats "because we have a young man who's going to come out and entertain you." At that moment, I asked myself why I was doing this. I wasn't ambitious. My life in New Orleans was perfectly fine. And yet . . .

"This can be your big break," Byron said.

"I know," I said. "But I'm scared to death."

"You're going to be fine," he said. "Just be yourself."

After a quick pass through makeup and a couple deep breaths to shake out my nervousness, I went onstage—my first time in front of multiple cameras, real lights, and an experienced director—where I sang a song and performed a monologue I had written. It seemed to go over well with the audience, but the only opinion that mattered belonged to the network executives watching from the booth, and I didn't see them afterward.

Later, over dinner, Byron analyzed my performance and expressed his belief that I had impressed the CBS brass. I was not as confident, though I didn't think I was terrible. I simply had no way of knowing, and that made me nervous.

The next morning, Byron took me into the vice president's office. He told me to relax, it was going to be a good meeting. He was right. The VP offered me a seven-year contract, with a starting salary of twenty thousand dollars a year—twice as much as I had made in my life.

I couldn't speak. I stared at the CBS executive, then at Byron, and kept going back and forth. Finally, Byron reached over to shake hands with the VP.

"Speaking on behalf of Dick, he accepts," he said. "As you can see, he is thrilled."

I nodded.

I was thrilled. Beyond thrilled. I was downright stunned. This was one of those proverbial big breaks, the kind you hear about, except it was happening to me, Dick Van Dyke, from Danville, Illinois.

While I went back home and gave my two weeks' notice, Byron rented us a house in Massapequa, a suburb on the South Shore of Long Island, and within the month, Margie and I and our three children had moved in. To celebrate our new good fortune, I took Margie on a Fifth Avenue shopping spree and we bought each other gifts as if we had just come into money. By our standards, we had.

Work-wise, I was assigned to the *CBS Morning Show*, airing Monday through Friday from seven to eight. Walter Cronkite hosted the show when it launched in 1954 as a two-hour broadcast. After Dave Garroway and NBC's *Today* show trounced it in the ratings, it was cut to sixty minutes, with the second hour going to *Captain Kangaroo*. Other hosts were brought in, including Jack Paar and Johnny Carson, then a lanky Midwestern comedian who was beginning his climb up TV's ranks.

The network also used humorist John Henry Faulk, whom I replaced after he was wrongly labeled a communist by a McCarthy-backed group and blacklisted from the business.

I wasn't aware of the reasons for Faulk's departure until later when he chronicled his ordeal in the wonderful book *Fear on Trial*. I walked into my new job as the *Morning Show*'s announcer wonderfully, blissfully ignorant—and quite late.

My first day was July 18, 1955. I woke up at four A.M. because I had to be at the studio at six for rehearsal and I had an hour's drive into the city. I got in our Chevy, started it up, heard a loud snap, crackle, pop, and was suddenly engulfed by smoke.

I leapt from the car and waited for the smoke to clear. I tried the ignition again. The car was dead, and I would be, too, if I didn't get going.

I took a cab to the train station and caught the train into Manhattan. It was my first time on the Long Island Rail Road, but I did not worry, as I still had plenty of time to get to work. It seemed like I might even save time, since I could get off at Grand Central Station, where, in fact, the studio was located, way up high in the upper floors above the terminal.

But in keeping with the way the day began, I missed my stop and ended up at Penn Station, on Seventh Avenue and Thirty-first Street. I was not even close. I checked my watch. It was time to panic. The cushion I had wanted before going on the air was virtually gone, and so was my sense of calm.

I hopped in a taxi and implored the driver to hurry to Grand Central. That may work in the movies, but in real life, as anyone who has driven in Manhattan knows, it's nearly impossible to hurry through crosstown traffic, and for some reason it becomes exponentially slower when time is a factor.

When I finally hurried into the studio, the show had already been on for twenty minutes. Merv Griffin, a young singer and a regular on the show until the format was changed a few months later, was filling in and proving that he was a much better emcee than I was ever going to be.

My bosses understood, though, and they hustled me on the air and let me keep my job. Live TV was like that. Every day you marched into the heart of the unknown, like one of those crazy people who purposely drive into the eye of a tornado. The only certainty was that something would go wrong, if not today, then tomorrow. It required nerves of steel and a sense of humor to match.

The mistakes were not funny when they happened, but afterward they had a way of seeming hilarious. The great Dixieland trumpet player Bill Davison showed up one morning so stoned that I had to prop him in the corner. I had to look back after we went off the air to make sure he wasn't still there. Guests came in all the time still drunk or stoned from the night before. I came to realize that that glassy-eyed look meant I was not only going to ask the questions but also have to figure out a way to come up with the answers.

My most memorable disaster occurred when I interviewed a dogsled racer. I was going to question him about traversing Canada's Laurentian Mountains. He had his team of dogs set up on the stage. They were gorgeous animals. Just before we went live, he warned, "Whatever you do, don't say 'mush' to the dogs."

"Okay," I told myself, and made a mental note. But of course during our interview, as I asked him about driving his team of dogs, I began clowning around and jokingly said, "Mush." It just came out of me. His dogs didn't understand it was a joke and they took off. They ran through the kitchen set, the weather set, and two other sets, knocking all of them down, before they stopped.

I never thought I was good at reading the news or interviewing the more serious-minded people who came into the studio. It wasn't my cup of tea. I got by only because my newsmen were two of the best who ever worked in television, Walter Cronkite and Charles Collingwood.

However, six months into the show, the network removed Walter. I guess they thought he was busy enough with the *Evening*

News and his own show, *You Are There,* but apparently that was not communicated to Walter. He called me as soon as he heard, looking for an explanation.

"What did I do?" he asked. "What didn't you like?"

"What are you talking about?" I asked.

"What did I do that got me fired?"

Walter was ten years older than I was, far more experienced, and basically in a whole other universe at the network. But I realized he had no idea what was going on. I set him straight.

"Walter, I can't fire anybody," I said. "I'm lucky to have this job myself."

My way out of the news and into a more comfortable role was to start doing a five-minute segment where I sat in front of a large easel, told famous children's stories and fairy tales, and illustrated them with cartoons. A composer named Hank Silvern wrote me a theme song called "Mice on Rollerskates." And viewers seemed to like the segment. But I went into work one morning and found all my belongings in the hall.

In short time, I learned that the network had brought in a new producer, Charlie Andrews, a nice guy who actually turned out to be quite helpful. But they had given him my office without telling me. I was assured that it wasn't a message; it was a mistake. I was also told not to read anything into the fact that they didn't have a place to put me.

Yet how could I not get upset? It was six in the morning and I was standing in the hall, without an office—and with a show to do.

I got on my high horse and complained to the network's vice president of television, Harry Amerly. It wasn't fair, I told him. In those days, CBS was known as the Tiffany network, and it was. Network headquarters was located at Fifty-second Street and Madison Avenue, the heart of Manhattan, and the executives were gentlemen. They dressed to the nines and conducted themselves accordingly. There wasn't any skulduggery. The network was run beautifully. And Harry reflected that sensibility. He responded to my ire by saying, "Let's go out to lunch."

He took me to Louie & Armond's, an upscale speakeasy on Fifty-second Street. I didn't drink at the time. Harry nevertheless ordered me a couple of martinis, one right after the other, which I sipped until I felt a chill in my extremities and heard Harry's voice begin to fade into the distance as he said something about getting me a new office.

"Boy, I don't feel well," I said, and then, all of a sudden, *boom!* My head hit the table. I passed out.

I never did get a new office, and after a year on the anchor desk, CBS took me off *The Morning Show.* I spent 1956 as host of the network's Saturday-morning *Cartoon Theater,* a series done on film where I interacted with Heckle and Jeckle and other popular characters. I was also a panelist on *To Tell the Truth,* which didn't go that well. Every night, the show's producers, Mark Goodson and Bill Todman, came in and shook hands with the three panelists—actually, not all three. They avoided me.

For some reason, they never acknowledged my presence. They didn't like me. I said to myself, "My career here is going to be rather short." I was not altogether wrong. Yet when they were working out the idea for a new game show called *The Price Is Right,* they had me emceeing it. We brought in people off the street and tried to figure out the show. I went home numerous nights and said to Margie, "This is the dumbest idea. People are just trying to guess how much things cost. That's a show? It's never going to go."

Despite my opinion, they got it off the ground, giving the

hosting job to Bill Cullen, and it became a TV staple. More than fifty years later, it's still going.

I then tried my hand at a few pilots that didn't work and bided my time as the network tried to figure out what to do with me.

They didn't try too hard. There was one executive, Oscar Katz, the vice president of programming, who was not a fan. He didn't think I had enough talent. In a meeting with other executives trying to find a place for me, he once said, "The kid just doesn't have it." I knew what he meant. At times, as I knocked around the network, I kind of agreed with him.

7

LAUGH LINES

It was the spring of 1958, and Garry Moore asked me to sub for him when he went on a month-long sailing vacation. That should have been a sign that I was on my way up at CBS. I had made numerous appearances on his show in the past, including one of my favorites, a skit with Chuck McCann featuring the two of us as Laurel and Hardy (me as Stan Laurel and Chuck as Oliver Hardy). But just as I began to find my comfort zone, two things happened that seemed to foreshadow my future at the network.

First, a zookeeper came on with an anteater, which relieved itself on the stage. It would have been funny if not for a noxious odor that quite simply stunk up the entire studio.

Then, on another show, I was chatting with Garry's sidekick, Durward Kirby, who pointed at someone in the audience. As I turned to look, his fingernail sliced into my nose. I bled like a pig.

Durward finished the show for me while I went offstage and got bandaged.

While my bleeding stopped, it was too late to save me at CBS. After a three-year run, they let me go. They said they didn't know what to do with me, and frankly, I didn't know what to do with me, either.

I drove home and told Margie that I had lost my job. My voice cracked several times as I relayed the details. She put on a good face, but I saw the concern in her eyes. I'm sure she saw the same in mine. I reminded her that we had been in worse spots, but it was really more for my benefit. With a wife and three children, and a house at the end of a cul-de-sac, I shouldered the responsibility of keeping everyone fed, warm, and feeling secure, and I was scared to death.

Around that same time, my agent set me up with a reporter who promised to do a little puff piece that would keep my name in circulation. The reporter asked me to describe my career goals.

"I want to eat," I said.

He laughed.

I wasn't joking.

I liked the life we had made for ourselves. Our neighborhood was full of families similar to us. The couples were young, upwardly mobile, with kids the same ages as ours. Everyone knew one another. Every Saturday night someone had a party. We had dinner, with a lot of drinking before and after, and played charades, which got pretty competitive. Once I got so wrapped up in the game that I broke out in hives.

Until this time, I didn't drink. Margie and I always kept a bottle of Early Times whiskey in the cupboard for company, but it went untouched for years. I began to enjoy a cocktail only as our social life picked up. I found a martini or two, and eventually three or four, got me past my shyness and helped me have a good time. And in those days, everybody drank and smoked and thought nothing of it. You were given odd looks if you didn't.

I taught Sunday school at the Dutch Reformed Presbyterian Church, and when I saw friends with whom I had partied the night before, I would roll my eyes and ask if they had recovered from the good times. I made it look sort of funny. It would not be as funny later on when I realized that I had a drinking problem. But that was still a long way off, and it was an even longer time before I understood it.

The drinking never interfered with the work, which picked up again when I landed a guest spot on *The Phil Silvers Show* as Sgt. Bilko's cousin. Then I was doing weekly pantomimes on *The Pat Boone Show* when I ran into Gil Cates, a young producer who went on to have an excellent career directing movies and producing TV, including more than a dozen Academy Awards telecasts.

Gil liked me. He was launching a daytime game show called *Mother's Day,* and he hired me to emcee. We shot at the famous Latin Quarter nightclub on Broadway and Forty-seventh Street. I stuck it out for an entire season because I needed the money, but unfortunately for both Gil and me, overseeing diaper-changing races and floor-mopping contests was not my thing.

I went on to host another game show called *Laugh Line.* On it, a group of actors struck a pose while a panel of funny people, including Mike Nichols, Elaine May, Shelley Berman, Orson Bean, and Dorothy Loudon, attempted to come up with a humorous description for it. With a panel full of comedy Hall of Famers, you'd think that show would still be on the air. But it didn't matter how funny those people were, and they were funny. The show didn't work.

And pretty soon, neither did I.

B ut the whole time I hosted those game shows, I hedged my bets against unemployment by auditioning for plays. As soon as I finished the show, I raced into the theater district. I was trying to expand my options as a performer. That's how I found out I could sing and dance. Sure, I had sung in high school and danced in some school plays, but I never considered doing it professionally. I was at one of those auditions and someone asked if I could sing and dance.

"Sure," I said.

Hey, fear of being hungry and homeless will do that to you.

I would have said yes to almost anything short of tightrope walking and then at least tried it.

As it happened, I could sing and dance some. I found that if I went with the music and just did what I felt, I could do pretty well.

Well enough, anyway.

I landed a little variety show with Peter Gennaro, the gifted dancer and choreographer (he'd collaborated with Jerome Robbins on the original Broadway production of *West Side Story*), and Ruth Price, who was eighteen and a knockout. The show closed after a very brief run, but Aaron Ruben, a writer-producer from *The Phil Silvers Show*, noticed my work and took a shine to me. He became a friend and supporter.

Aaron and I began palling around together, working out at the Y and talking over coffee. Eleven years older than I was, he had written for George Burns, Milton Berle, Phil Silvers, and Sid Caesar, and would go on to co-create *The Andy Griffith Show* and

Gomer Pyle, U.S.M.C. Some people have the magic touch, and he was one of them. He promised to look out for possible jobs for me, and when he started doing the company sketches for *Girls Against the Boys,* a comedy revue, he got me in as part of the chorus, as well as in short pieces between scene changes.

The show starred Bert Lahr, Nancy Walker, and Shelley Berman. Aaron warned that "these people were hysterical," and he was right. Bert could just look at the audience and get laughs, and Nancy knew when to do those kind of takes, too. I had one sketch with Nancy set in a deli in which I played a married man meeting up with a girl, and Nancy was the deli owner who attempts to distract me from the girl with her chopped liver.

It was funny, but after eating chopped liver eight times a week, I got nauseous just thinking about eating it.

Aaron also helped me write a pantomime of a guy who came home very drunk, but the second his wife appeared, he was as sober as a judge. Every time she turned her head, though, he was drunk again. The pacing kept speeding up, and so did the antics. I got a lot of laughs—and a good review.

In early November 1959, after workshopping the show in Philadelphia, we moved to Broadway. Despite some relatively good notices and a Hirschfeld cartoon in the *New York Times, Girls Against the Boys* was too light to compete with the drama-heavy season that included Mary Martin in *The Sound of Music,* Patty Duke in *The Miracle Worker,* and John Gielgud in *Much Ado About Nothing,* and the show closed after a mere two weeks.

But that was enough time for me to impress noted choreographer Danny Daniels, who introduced himself to me after the opening and said, "Boy, I've never seen anybody move like you do." He and Aaron got me on *The Fabulous Fifties,* a TV special celebrating the decade that was just about to end. In one sketch, I played a shy wallflower-type who learns to mambo, but then goes to a nightclub where everyone is doing the cha-cha. So he returns to the dance studio, learns the cha-cha, and then finds everyone at the club doing the Frug. So he learns the Frug, and so on. It was nonstop—and on live television. I had to dance twelve minutes straight. I almost died from exhaustion.

Aaron also put me into the lead of *The Trouble with Richard,* a pilot for CBS that we shot at an abandoned hotel in Lower Manhattan. I played a simpleminded bank teller who lived with his two aunts and infused the character with traits I had loved in Stan Laurel. But the network passed. As I recall, they said that "it looked cheap."

Disappointed, I phoned my agent at MCA, hoping he had some prospects. He put me on *Mike Stokey's Pantomime Quiz,* a charades-like TV game show that had been running since the late 1940s. I was partnered with Howard Morris and series regular Carol Burnett, whom I knew from working together on *The Garry Moore Show,* and that turned out to be a lucky break.

Carol and I were dynamos as teammates on *Pantomime Quiz.* Our personalities clicked, and so did our competitive juices. Thanks to a slew of imperceptible hand signals we came up with to tip each other off—some impromptu, some we worked out away from the show—we were unbeatable. It was a good thing, too. I needed the two hundred dollars we were paid each time we won to buy groceries.

My prospects brightened considerably when I learned that my agent had booked an audition with Gower Champion for another Broadway show. Champion was an actor turned director who had won a Tony Award a few years earlier for *Lend an Ear,* the show that made Carol Channing a star, and from what my agent told me, he was getting set to stage another musical, called *Bye Bye Birdie*. My agent said he had a good feeling about this one.

What he didn't tell me—perhaps he didn't know—was that Aaron Ruben had already been in there, on the inside, with Gower, laying the groundwork for me. He also smelled a hit and thought I was perfect for a key part as a songwriter-agent.

8

BYE BYE BIRDIE

My audition took place in a dimly lit, empty theater off Broadway, somewhere in the Forties. It was an overcast winter day. I walked into the theater and took off my jacket; I wore a sweater and khakis. There were only a few people there, including Gower, a handsome, serious man. It looked and felt how I imagine most people picture a Broadway audition—dark, austere, tense, and scary.

Gower and his producers sat at a table in front. I stayed in the back until I heard my name, then took my place on the stage. There was one light shining down and a piano player on the side.

After answering a few questions, I sang "Till There Was You" from *The Music Man* and then "Once in Love with Amy" with a little soft-shoe that I knew. When I finished, Gower came onstage and said, "You've got the part." Just like that. He gave me the job. Right on the spot.

I didn't know what the hell to say, and what I eventually said sounded completely wrong.

"But I . . . I can't really dance."

"Don't worry about that," he said. "I saw what you *can* do. That's what we'll build on. I'll teach you to dance."

Those lessons paid off handsomely. With a book by Michael Stewart and music and lyrics from Charles Strouse and Lee Adams, respectively, *Birdie* was a takeoff on the mania that swept through the youth of America when Elvis Presley was drafted into the Army in 1958. After I saw a run-through of the number "Telephone Hour," I called my wife and told her that this show was going to go and probably do very well. It felt like everything worked.

From day one, the show had a special feel, at least among those of us on the inside, a remarkable cast featuring Dick Gautier as Conrad Birdie, Susan Watson as Kim MacAfee, Paul Lynde as her father, Kay Medford as my mother, Chita Rivera as my assistant, Rosie Alvarez, and me in the role of agent and songwriter Albert Peterson. Michael J. Pollard played the kid, Hugo, and Charles Nelson Reilly was Mr. Henkel, in addition to my understudy.

We rehearsed at the Phyllis Anderson Theater on Fourteenth Street, near the great old German restaurant Luchow's, in the heart of what had once been the Yiddish theater district. Chita and I met on the first day of rehearsals and instantly hit it off. Both of us were clowns and made each other laugh. Gower sent us home one day after we couldn't stop ourselves from laughing. He was a quiet man and under a lot of stress from directing and choreographing the show, and he just snapped.

"Just go home!" he said.

We left the theater like naughty schoolchildren, laughing

even though we knew nothing was funny. I thought we were going to get fired.

I lucked out being able to dance with Chita. She was a natural, a whiz-bang genuine crowd-pleaser. I didn't have to do much of anything except move with her, and as a result, I ended up looking like Fred Astaire. Her husband, Tony Mordente, later spotlighted in *West Side Story,* was understudying the role of Birdie and assisting Gower, and he grew jealous of how chummy Chita and I became.

He was jealous of any guy who got near Chita or gave her a look. He blew up if a cabdriver said something to her. All of a sudden he got the idea Chita and I were stepping out on him, and one day he confronted me. For a moment I thought he might kill me.

"Are you crazy?" I said. "I don't do that."

Luckily he believed me and we all stayed good friends.

One night, just before we left town to workshop the show in Philadelphia, I exited the theater and started down the snow-covered sidewalk on Fourteenth Street when a tall, skinny guy came up to me and said, "Excuse me, do you have a dresser yet?"

I looked up—and up—and immediately recognized one of the tallest people I knew: Frank Adamo. A fairly recent acquaintance, he had recently lost his job as a junior ad executive at the J. Walter Thompson agency, and he was looking for something else, something different.

"I don't know," I said. "What's a dresser?"

I really didn't know.

When I had done *Girls Against the Boys* the previous year I didn't know that theater people did their own makeup. On the first night, I asked someone to point me toward the makeup room.

They laughed and explained that I had to do it myself. That night, I borrowed makeup from some people and went out looking like Emmett Kelly the clown.

Frank smiled.

"Sure," he said. "A dresser is the person who takes care of your wardrobe, makes sure it's clean and hung up and ready for you every night. I'll also do all the other things you will need done."

"Oh, I see," I said.

"I also need a job," he said matter-of-factly.

"Well, you got one," I said. "We're opening at the Shubert Theater in Philadelphia."

"Yes, I know," he said.

"Then I'll see you there."

We shook hands, and the next time I saw Frank was in Philadelphia where he had my clothes hung up in my dressing room, as promised. Somehow he intuitively knew I was particular about my clothes. He also took care of everything else. He was so good, in fact, that he ended up staying with me for years, later serving as my secretary and stand-in on *The Dick Van Dyke Show*. And later still, he worked for Mary Tyler Moore.

Philadelphia was where the show came together and I got to know my talented castmates, and they were a brilliant lot, starting with Gower and my pal Chita. Then there was Paul Lynde. No one has ever played the part of Mr. MacAfee like him. My God, he was funny, just off-the-charts funny, but he was also very prickly. He made it known that he didn't want anyone stepping on his lines, and God help those who did. He could be vicious.

Michael J. Pollard was a sweetheart, though on matinee days he went out between shows and got a little tipsy, and invariably, not long before the second show, I'd hear a knock on my dressing room door, and there would be Michael, his smile just a little off, his eyes glazed, wanting to know what was going on. I didn't even have to ask. I knew that he was plastered.

I brewed him some coffee, threw him in the shower, and he was fine by showtime. If he wasn't, I never knew the difference.

I was especially fond of my understudy, Charles Nelson Reilly. I hadn't met anyone quite like him, but I took to him instantly. He was hysterically funny, clever, quick, and intelligent. I was never bored around him. On the first night of previews, it was raining and he came into my dressing room with a scarf around his head and purred, "Hello, my name is Eve Harrington. I'm such a fan of your work."

He did the whole scene from *All About Eve*, which put me on the floor. He was one of a kind.

The truth is, I owed everything to Gower, who put me in the show and then gave me the benefit of his time, talent, and creative eye. I can't tell you what he saw in me as a singer and dancer, but he saw something, and then he made the most of it, or rather enabled me to make the most of it. As a dancer, I was strictly an amateur. Yet he taught me tricks and moves that not only added to my ability and repertoire but also made me more comfortable, and that was key.

Singing was another matter. I could carry a tune. That much I'll say. But I was not a good singer. Dick Gautier, who had the title role as Conrad Birdie, was the same way. Both of us learned that you can't sing incorrectly eight times a week without getting hoarse. We had a scene where he came downstairs holding a beer and I said, "Hi, Conrad. How are you doing?" Between the two of us, we barely managed to eke out a sound.

It wasn't really funny, but it was to us, and we laughed. Others weren't as amused, though. Unbeknownst to me, during previews, the show's producers didn't think I was cutting it. I probably wasn't; not then, anyway. They wanted to replace me, but Gower stepped in and asked for more time.

"Look, he's going to be all right," he said. "Let me work with him."

He had an idea. He put the writers to work and overnight they came back with a revised version of the song "Put On a Happy Face," which they had originally written for Chita. But Gower gave it to me, explaining, "The skinny kid doesn't have anything to do in the first act. Give it to him."

Of course, that song changed my life.

The show opened in New York at the Martin Beck Theater on April 14, 1960. I was a nervous wreck all day and into the evening before the show. I brought Margie and the kids into the city and we got adjoining rooms at the Algonquin Hotel. Despite my nervousness, the performance could not have gone better. We heard nothing but enthusiastic applause after each song and a long, foot-stomping ovation at the end.

It felt like a hit, and it was—even though the *New York Times'* venerable critic Brooks Atkinson chided the show's folksy simplicity and called some scenes "ludicrous." But he praised Dick Gautier and Paul Lynde. My role puzzled him. "Mr. Van Dyke is a likeable comedian, who has India-rubber joints; and Miss Rivera is a flammable singer and gyroscopic dancer." But, as he put it, our scenes "have little relevance to the main business of the evening."

As a group of us read the review together in Sardi's that night, we wondered if he had seen the same show we had performed. Apparently the critic had the same sense, too. "Last evening, the audience was beside itself with pleasure," he wrote at the close of the piece. "This department was able to contain itself."

A short time into the run, the production moved from the Martin Beck to the 54th Street Theater. By then I had grown comfortable in the part and was bringing much more to it than the *New York Times'* critic had seen on opening night. I had also fallen into a nice daily routine. I went home after the show, then spent the next day relaxing until I went into the city, usually in time to have an early dinner at Sardi's. I loved their cannelloni. On matinee days, I had it for both lunch and dinner.

During intermission one night, my wife called me. She was frantic. Our ten-year-old son, Chris, had run away and she couldn't find him. She thought he had been kidnapped. I was distracted the whole second act; two-thirds of my brain was thinking about something else the whole time I was onstage. I raced home after the show and found police cars in the driveway and cops and bloodhounds searching through the woods behind our backyard.

They found Chris sound asleep under a tree, oblivious to the surrounding panic. It turned out that he'd had an argument with his younger brother, Barry, and my wife had sided with Barry, a decision that Chris thought was unfair. So he decided the hell with such injustice, and he ran into the woods.

From then on, I knew that boy was going to be a handful—and I turned out to be right. But he was always a good kid, and eventually he became a lawyer, a good one, too—the state district attorney in Salem, Oregon, in fact.

In some ways, those sorts of interruptions of the normal routine weren't unusual. There was one night, for example, when I got caught in a blizzard on my drive into Manhattan and never made it to the theater. I had left home a little later than usual, after having an early dinner with Margie and the kids, and about halfway into the city, my Corvette ran into an enormous snowdrift. It was snowing hard, almost whiteout conditions, and the highway was no longer navigable.

I wasn't the only one who got stuck, either. There were a few of us, and we got out of our cars, nodded and said hi, and started walking. I wasn't that bundled up, and along with a couple of others, we thought we might freeze to death in the biting wind and snow.

We came to a restaurant, though, one of those diners right off the highway, and went inside. A bunch of other people had also taken shelter there. Making the show became moot. I spent the night in a booth, drinking coffee, talking, and waiting for the storm to let up.

The next morning, I caught a ride back home on a snowplow. The snow didn't stop for days, and then it took a couple more before it began to melt. When I finally went back to get my Corvette, I found it in two pieces. A snowplow had come along and blindly cut it in half.

During one show, I looked out and recognized Fred Astaire out front, in the house seats. He was one of my idols. Imagine trying to dance in front of Fred Astaire. I had a long moment when I thought my so-called India-rubber legs might not only freeze mid-dance, but actually walk offstage on their own accord and refuse to go back on.

Another night we were told Cary Grant was in the house. I couldn't see him during the performance, but afterward I was in my dressing room and there was a knock on the door. I opened it up, and there was Cary Grant. When I saw him, I prayed my eyes didn't betray my surprise. Before I could think of what to say to him, he pushed me aside and started going through my closet. I wore my own suits in the show, some of which were tailored and quite handsome, and my assistant, Frank, had hung them neatly.

"These are very nice," he said.

"Thank you," I said. "Actually, I was given the After Six Award as the best-dressed on Broadway."

"Well done, young man," he said.

Years later, Cary asked me to do a movie with him, one of those Doris Day–type romantic comedies, and I declined. I don't know what the hell was the matter with me. I could have worked with Cary Grant. Thank goodness I had better sense when Carl Reiner came to the show and offered me the role that changed my life.

9

ROB AND LAURA PETRIE

I n his book *My Anecdotal Life,* Carl Reiner called me "the finest all-around performer to ever grace a situation comedy," so it's only appropriate that I take a moment to return the compliment by saying that in the history of television, Carl is the finest all-around writer to ever create a situation comedy. He's also one of the finest human beings to do so.

But that represents only a fraction of my admiration for this very funny, intelligent, and kind man.

Long before I met him, Carl was already among my heroes. I worshipped the Bronx-born comedy genius as a mainstay on *Your Show of Shows,* the classic variety series starring Sid Caesar and Imogene Coca. Airing on NBC from 1950 to 1954, it also featured Howard Morris and Nanette Fabray. Carl, though a regular performer, also considered himself one of the writers, an illustrious bunch that included Mel Brooks, Neil Simon, his brother Danny, and head writer Mel Tolkin.

Each season was thirty-nine weeks, and the show was broadcast live for ninety minutes. It was understandable why Sid would get a little crazy whenever people asked him how many retakes they did. The answer was: none. There weren't any second takes. They had one chance every week, and they had to get that sucker as perfect as possible the first time.

The show was a milestone in TV comedy, and in the summer of 1959, it inspired Carl, who won two Emmy Awards for Best Supporting Actor during that period, to write a sitcom based on his experiences as a writer there.

At the time, Carl was living with his wife, Estelle, and their three children in New Rochelle, New York. He went off to Fire Island and wrote his first sitcom script. He called it *Head of the Family*. Being a visionary and a prolific storyteller, he didn't stop with that one script, either. He wrote thirteen episodes—one-third of an entire season!

Then he shot a pilot starring himself as TV writer Rob Petrie and Barbara Britton as his wife, Laura. He cast Sylvia Miles and Morty Gunty as his writing partners on the fictional *Alan Sturdy Show,* and he put actor Jack Wakefeld in the role of Alan Sturdy. CBS liked the pilot, but not enough. However, they did respond to Carl, who was advised to try again.

As he regrouped, Carl was introduced to Sheldon Leonard, a brilliant TV producer with a Midas touch. His credits already included two classics, *The Danny Thomas Show* and *The Andy Griffith Show.* After viewing the original pilot, Sheldon, like everyone else, became an instant and devoted fan of Carl's writing. He also made a suggestion, not an easy one, either, considering the stature of the person to whom he was making it.

He told Carl the show needed to be recast.

And Carl—did I also mention he was one of the wisest men to ever create a situation comedy?—understood.

He also agreed to let Sheldon direct the pilot, which, in retrospect, was like Babe Ruth welcoming Lou Gehrig into the lineup. Or something like that. The two of them were superstars, and Carl knew Sheldon's sensibility and experience were only going to help this project that was so personal to him.

I say God bless both of them—and thank you—because in thinking about who should play Rob Petrie, Sheldon recalled seeing me in *Girls Against the Boys,* and he came to the theater to see me in *Birdie.* A short time later, he returned with Carl, with both of them looking at me as their lead actor.

I had no idea they were in the audience and neither man came backstage afterward. But later I heard that Carl had been very entertained and impressed, and he left the theater thinking that I was the right guy.

Over the years, I have heard and read about other actors they considered, including Johnny Carson. I have also heard and read various accounts of why they liked me. My favorites? I wasn't too good-looking, I walked a little funny, and I was basically kind of average and ordinary.

I guess my lack of perfection turned out to be a winning hand. Let that be a lesson for future generations.

Through my agent, I received eight scripts from Carl—the first eight scripts of this new series that didn't have a title or any actors. No longer called *Head of the Family,* Carl had rewritten each episode, not that it would have mattered to me. I hadn't read the originals. I'm sure they were as brilliant as those sent to me. The eight I read were magnificent. They were fresh and funny. They resonated with real-life energy and insights that I recognized from my own life and the lives of people I knew. Carl was dialed in, as they say.

I read one after another eager to see what was next. Midway through, I turned to Margie and said, "My God, this guy is good."

It's one of the great understatements in TV history.

He was Carl Reiner.

So no one accuses me of venturing into hyperbole, let me say there were no one-liners in these scripts, no corny or cheap jokes for the sake of comedy. The humor grew out of the people and their relationships to one another and their jobs. It was organic, natural, real, and timeless. I keep going back to the same point, but anyone who has been in a hit TV series will mention the same thing as the essential ingredient. It was the writing. It was fantastic.

"I want to do this," I told my agent. "What's next?"

Next, I met with Carl. He offered me the job and asked me to fly to Los Angeles to make the pilot. Part of me was ready to go right away, but I had some reservations about leaving a hit play and uprooting my family from a place where we'd grown very comfortable. In my meeting with Carl I found myself working out this conflict perhaps subconsciously by telling him about an idea I had for a series that I was calling *Man on a Scooter.*

Inspired by the great physical comedy of Jacques Tati's 1953 movie *Les Vacances de Monsieur Hulot,* I envisioned myself playing an associate professor from a small Ohio college who takes a sabbatical and travels through Europe with his typewriter on the back of a Vespa, having one adventure after another.

I had already pitched it to a network and a few producers without any interest, and Carl reacted like everyone else, only kinder. He said that while he, too, admired Tati, he thought my idea was a movie, not a TV series.

"It's one idea," he said, and a TV series, he explained, had to have an infinite number of story ideas, like real life—and like his scripts about Rob and Laura Petrie, their son, Ritchie, Rob's coworkers Sally Rogers and Buddy Sorrell, their boss, Mel Cooley, and their neighbors Jerry and Millie Helper.

After getting a week off from *Birdie,* I flew to Los Angeles and met with Sheldon Leonard and Carl in Carl's second-floor office at Desilu Studios. I had signed on for $1,500 an episode, and I was very excited. I felt like I was a little twig on the Sid Caesar family tree; I was honored and thrilled to have any sort of attachment to that comedy lineage. Once we began to work, I was not only honored and thrilled, but I was also impressed.

Sheldon and Carl had already cast Rose Marie as Sally Rogers, and she had told Carl about Morey Amsterdam, who was also hired, to play the role of Buddy Sorrell. Both were comedy veterans. As for Mary, it's well-known that Sheldon and Carl considered dozens of actresses before settling on Mary Tyler Moore, a young actress whose previous work, outside of commercials and dancing, was playing a receptionist on the series *Richard Diamond, Private Detective,* though her great legs were all that anyone ever saw of her.

But plenty of other people in town had seen her, including Danny Thomas, one of our executive producers and one of Hollywood's biggest, smartest stars on his own. She had auditioned to play his daughter on *Make Room for Daddy,* better known as *The Danny Thomas Show,* but as Carl later quipped, "She missed it by a nose." Indeed, as Danny added, "No daughter of mine could ever have a nose that small."

But he suggested "the girl with three names" to Carl, and

she got the role. Her nose was perfect, as was she. Everyone loved Mary.

What wasn't to love? I adored her from the moment we were introduced. I think both of us had each other at hello. But I still had a couple of problems. For one, I thought she was too young to play my wife. She was twelve years younger than I was, though as time went by, no one ever noticed or mentioned that fact. Even I forgot about it. Then, during our initial read-throughs of the first episode, titled "The Sick Boy and the Sitter," I was concerned that Mary wasn't much of a comedienne.

It is hard to imagine. But she was stiff and proper, polite. She didn't seem to have much of a funny bone. I saw a little Katharine Hepburn in her, but not much Lucille Ball.

Of course, I was wrong. And therein is yet another reason Carl was known as a genius and I was referred to as "the actor playing Rob Petrie." Within a few days of reading and working together—really in no time at all—Mary got it. With Carl, Rosie, and Morey in the room, she had the best teachers. These people knew comedy like nobody else. They had funny in their bones, down into the marrow. On top of that, they had impeccable timing. Mine was pretty good, too. And Mary was the A-plus student. She absorbed everything—the chemistry, the rhythm—and emerged a comedienne herself.

I had never seen a transformation like hers, and I still haven't. She went from black to white. The first time I stood across from her in rehearsal and heard her say, "Oh, Rob!" I thought, That's it, we're home.

All of a sudden, she was perfect.

Little Cahuenga Studios, or Little Desilu, became our home away from home. We spent much of that first week as a cast preparing for the pilot by sitting around a table, reading the script, and throwing out suggestions as Carl listened and wrote. He was brought up on *Your Show of Shows,* where they sat around the table and threw out lines. We did the same. Everybody got to suggest dialogue and work out their parts, and Carl wrote and, more accurately, rewrote the scripts as he fine-tuned each role to our personalities, strengths, speech patterns, and inflections.

Imagine humming a tune to Mozart. With perfect pitch, something I still marvel at, he captured every one of us. It made it so we didn't have to act. All we had to do was read our parts. We were playing ourselves.

We had to hold Morey down. He was an encyclopedia with a million jokes in his head. They popped out of him at a rapid-fire pace, and they were hiliarious, except most didn't fit the story. He wasn't always wrong, though. Sometimes he threw in a great one, and Carl kept it.

Carl was like that with all of us. If someone offered a line and it was funny and fit the story, it stayed in. That was the ethos as we worked on the pilot, and it stayed that way for the entire run of the series.

I liked everyone instantly and the feeling was mutual. We all liked one another and everyone had a handle on the idea. Throughout the week, we knew we were headed in the right direction. The show got better, funnier, and each of us grew more comfortable in our parts. That was when I was at my most creative, when I was on the set, doing the work. With the adrenaline flowing, you never knew what might happen.

I was so nervous before taping the pilot that fever blisters broke out in my mouth. That morning we were to begin taping, I looked in the mirror and counted five of them. I thought, Poor

Mary, I have to kiss her in the opening scene when I come home from work excited because my boss, Alan Brady, has invited us to a party at his penthouse home. We shot the pilot on January 21, 1961, the same day John F. Kennedy was sworn in as the thirty-fifth president of the United States, in front of three cameras and a live audience, just like present-day sitcoms do, and got laughs in all the right places, and even a few unexpected places. Toward the end, there was a big party scene at Alan's house where everyone got to perform, and it went flawlessly, too.

Everything worked, including ideas we had discussed earlier and little impromptu bits that came to us in the moment. We came off as a married couple. It was thrilling. I could tell it was working, and so could Mary. From the start, we had a special timing and chemistry that you can't manufacture. It's either there or it isn't. With us, it was there—and it only got better over time.

All of us were learning. I spoke to Carl between takes about the shadings of my character. We had been discussing Rob throughout the week and continued the conversation every chance we had. Carl had a picture in his head, and I was just getting acquainted with him. The two would quickly merge, his vision and my portrayal, and then the fun really started.

He knew that I loved physical comedy, so we made Rob a tad klutzy. If he could trip or bump into something at an inopportune or unlikely moment, he did. It was during one of the early rehearsals that I came up with the idea to stumble over the living room ottoman, which became a signature of the show's opening. I tried it and Carl laughed—especially at my expression. It was golden.

Everything about Rob was like that. He was relatable. A comedy writer may not be familiar to everyone, but he was a husband

and father, a good guy who tried hard to make sure things went right, that he did a good job, and that he not get flustered when things went awry. I was able to pour so much of myself into him before I even knew I was doing that. Like me, he hated confrontation. Carl had a deft eye for piling up intricate little problems that turned into challenges that thwarted Rob, including his job, his coworkers, his roles as a husband and a responsible provider, and his own charming, well-intentioned self. Every time he came up with a new situation that caused Laura to wince, "Oh, Rob!" I thought, Oh, good, this is going to be fun.

It was also no accident that we had numerous episodes with parties where we broke into song or dance. All of us looked for any excuse to perform, and Carl relished any and every opportunity to write in a number, since they shortened the script by ten pages or so.

As we shot the pilot, I mispronounced Rob and Laura's last name, saying *Pet-re* rather than *Pee-tree,* as Carl had done in the original when he based the name on some actual neighbors of his in New Rochelle. Nobody corrected me, and so it stuck.

Another name stuck, too—the show's title.

That was the problem the whole time we began working on the remake. There wasn't a title. No one wanted to use the old name, *Head of the Family.* Carl came up with numerous suggestions, one more clever than the next, but none of them hit the magic note that made Carl and Sheldon go, "Aha, that's it!"

Ideas were pitched all week and just as quickly dismissed, including *Double Trouble,* which Sheldon championed, as it was his idea.

But Carl shook his head. Our conductor heard it as a sour note.

"The problem is we have a show with a star that no one has

heard of," Carl said. "We need something that will make both Dick and the show a household name."

One afternoon, with time running out before we had to deliver a title to CBS, Sheldon, an imposing, opinionated man who was always perfectly dressed, fit, and tan, as well as a man who possessed an impressive vocabulary and used it to his advantage, got into a discussion with Carl, who had his own arsenal of opinions and arguments. As they went back and forth, Carl suggested calling it *The Dick Van Dyke Show*. I saw his face brighten.

"Look, *Make Room for Daddy,* a big hit, became better known as *The Danny Thomas Show*," Carl said. "We should do the same. It solves our problems."

Sheldon, who looked as if someone had just put a pinch of bitters on his tongue, didn't think so.

"*The Dick Van Dyke Show*," he said slowly, as if placing it on a shelf and standing back to assess how it looked.

All of a sudden everyone looked. All eyes swung to me. I wanted to hide. Rosie, appearing more perplexed than anyone, shook her head and said, "What's a Dick Van Dyke?"

I agreed. It sounded like a mistake.

"Nobody's ever heard of me," I said. "Who's going to tune in?"

"I disagree," Carl said. "I think it's perfect."

10

SHOWTIME

Less than a month after shooting the pilot, Carl called me at home in New York. I was reading the paper before going to the theater, but I immediately put it down when I heard the excitement in his voice. CBS had loved the pilot, he said, adding, they were picking it up for an entire season and we were going to get started as soon as I got to Los Angeles.

I am not even sure how I got through that night's performance of *Birdie*. I hung up with Carl and danced around the living room with Margie, who was pregnant with our fourth child. I don't remember exactly where I was later, whether I was standing outside our house before getting into the car to drive into the city or had paused next to the artists' entrance at the theater, staring up at the New York skyline, but I do remember feeling blessed, like something greater than me was happening, and yet, it was happening to me.

I planned nothing.

This was my lucky life.

We put our house up for sale and I gave notice at the play. The timing was perfect. I was only signed to the play for a year and that contract was just about up. My final performance in *Birdie* came in April 1961. It was a bittersweet night, as expected. The little girls with whom I sang "Put On a Happy Face" had tears running down their rosy cheeks, and Chita, who had become a dear friend, and I cried onstage, not caring if anyone in the audience noticed.

Two months later, I was buried in work on the TV series but still making news in the play. Apparently I won a Tony Award for Featured Actor. I say apparently because I had no idea that I was among the night's winners, which included Richard Burton for *Camelot,* Joan Plowright for *A Taste of Honey,* Zero Mostel for *Rhinoceros,* and Gower Champion for *Birdie.* Charles Nelson Reilly accepted the award on my behalf.

"Dick says thank you," he quipped. "And since he can't be here, I'd like to sing a few of my hits."

He had such a good time that night in my stead that he forgot to call and let me know the good news. No one else called, either. Notification did finally arrive via a congratulatory telegram, but somehow it ended up under the welcome mat outside our front door, and days passed before our housekeeper found it when she swept the front porch.

Oh, well.

As much as I loved New York, it was in the past. We had settled into a new house in Mandeville Canyon, a secluded Brentwood neighborhood close to the kids' schools. Byron Paul, who was managing my career, had gone ahead of us, bought a home for his family and then found one for ours two doors down from his. Our move went smoothly, except for my poor Chrysler, which I had put on the train in perfect running condition. It was dead on arrival, though.

I marveled at my kids, whose lives were unfolding in a very different manner than mine. Whereas I had been brought up in a small town surrounded by relatives, they had lived in Atlanta, New York, and now L.A. But they were great kids: smart, respect-ful, studious, adaptable, generous, and well-adjusted. I was more proud of them than anything else I had ever done.

Plus, as the little bump in Margie's belly attested, we had one more on the way that fall.

All of us adored L.A. It was warm and beautiful. Life was lived outdoors. None of us had any problems adjusting, not that I remember, but when minor issues with the children did arise, I simply turned to Carl and his wife, Estelle, both of whom were attuned to the latest advice in child-rearing. Actually, I turned to Carl whenever I had a question on any topic.

Over the years, I have accepted numerous awards and made sure to thank Carl. In fact, on more than one occasion, I can recall thanking Carl for my life. It always gets a laugh. But it's never been a joke. It's true. In addition to all his show-business smarts, he has always been someone with genuine wisdom about life. The two don't necessarily go hand in hand. With Carl, they did. When he put me in his show, he literally changed my entire life.

I only saw him lose his temper once and by then we were already a few years into the show. It was during rehearsal, early in the week, and we were playing around too much with a bad script, trying to fix it. Carl came to the set to watch a run-through and raised hell because we not only failed to fix the script, but we had, he said, made it worse as well.

Aside from that, the man was a model of hard work and

comedy genius who was determined to do things right from day one, and he did. He set the tone, wrote the scripts, and the rest of us enjoyed the ride of our lives.

Our first season, like all the others, was both effortless and joyful. I didn't have to be at the studio until ten A.M., so I was able to spend time with Margie and the kids before I made the thirty-minute drive to the Little Desilu studio in Hollywood. My workweek began on Wednesdays with a read-through of the new script. We all sat around a table, read lines, shared opinions, and tossed out new ideas. It was the beginning of a process that didn't stop until we got in front of the audience and shot the episode the following Tuesday, and even then we still added lines.

Carl was firmly in charge, but it was such a sharing environment, one where everyone knew the goal was to make the best and funniest episode possible, that we all felt comfortable voicing thoughts to that end. At the table, Carl took to calling me "Doc." It was always good-natured and casual. I didn't get it, though. We were halfway into the season when I finally told him that. He explained that everyone on *Your Show of Shows* had called Neil Simon by that name, Doc.

"He was a great writer, but quiet," said Carl. "All of us in the writers' room would be yelling and Neil would mention an idea, but no one could hear him. I'd say, 'Wait a minute, Doc's got something.' I made it a point to sit next to him so I could hear him."

The same thing happened on our show. I would throw out a line, but not loud enough to be heard over Sheldon, Morey, Rosie, Jerry Paris, or the others. But Carl would raise his hand to quiet the table and say, "Hey, Doc has got something."

Jerry Paris had ideas, too. A student of comedy, he possessed all the talents that can't be taught—timing, a sharp eye, and an intuitive sense for what worked. He was also one of those people who did not have an edit button. He said whatever he thought. Usually it was funny, but he pissed off his share of people. Jerry had acted for years, but he was more interested in directing. In preparation, he observed everything. Nothing happened on the set that Jerry did not know about or have an opinion on.

Before the end of the second season, he would get his chance, and then in the 1970s go on to even greater heights directing *Happy Days*. But during the first season of *The Dick Van Dyke Show* we all were obedient soldiers. Sheldon directed the pilot and then John Rich took over the rest of the season and much of the following one. John epitomized the value and purpose of a director, especially on a sitcom. Blessed with a marvelous sense of the ridiculous, he was brilliant at seeing all the possibilities in a scene. I did whatever hit me instinctively as I read the script. I never thought about another way to play a scene. John only thought about other ways.

He worked from a rolling lectern that he leaned on or gripped with his hands as we worked. His script was poised on top. A cigar was usually in his mouth. When he got upset—and he has a ferocious temper—John hit the lectern and chomped on his cigar. I braced myself for a thunderclap whenever I saw his cigar bouncing up and down. But when something worked, John laughed his head off.

Even with personalities as strong and persuasive as Sheldon and John, it was still always Carl's show. If it was funny, Carl's ear, as well as his office door, were always open. He was a first-rate collaborator. But he was the maestro and we were his orchestra. He had the final word.

On Mondays, we came in and spent all day blocking for the camera. It was the most boring day of the week, but it added to the anticipation of Tuesday, the day we performed the show. We arrived at one P.M. and did a run-through of the show, which I felt was when I did my best thinking. For me, that's when the magic happened, when the funny bones took over.

After rehearsal, we broke for dinner. While we ate, the audience came in. Then we did the show. By that point, I knew it was good and couldn't wait to get out there and show them what we had. Mary took a few weeks to get used to performing in front of an audience. She hadn't done that before. But soon she was like everyone else—chomping at the bit, excited.

On taping nights, Carl always greeted the audience with some lighthearted banter and got them laughing. Then he brought out Morey to further warm them up. That was always dicey. Morey knew as many jokes as anyone I ever met, but if he saw someone in the audience of a distinct ethnicity, his brain turned to that page of jokes in his head and he rattled off one after the other without thinking that he might be offending someone.

Those were delicate times compared to today, so I would often be backstage with the others, wincing at some of his jokes and praying we didn't have a problem. We never did. But we had other problems. Though it might seem quaint now, the network's censors had a problem with Mary's Capri pants. They thought they were too tight, and that turned into a bit of a battle, which Carl eventually won. Following the show's October 3, 1961, debut, I am sure Mary helped to sell Capri pants across the country.

The attention that Mary got didn't sit well with Rosie. She had come on board thinking the focus was going to be on the comedy writers and the TV show Rob worked on. She felt Mary's part should be a more minor one, at least as the role of wife was thought of in those prefeminist days, meaning she should serve more as window dressing to Rob's glitzier life in show business. However, Carl made it clear that the show was about both of

Rob's lives, work and home, and that the marriage was the foundation for everything else. Indeed, Rosie came to understand that the show worked just fine as it was.

From the outset, Carl envisioned a show that would be timeless. He wanted it to be fresh to audiences fifty years down the line. It was such a bold, confident vision, and correct. To that end, he made sure the scripts never contained references to the period. In other words, no politics, no slang, no mention of popular TV shows, films, or songs. In their place, he emphasized work, family, friendships, and human nature.

Carl was the master of knowing the difference between funny and not funny, but occasionally Sheldon took exception and the two of them got into a discussion that typically had them meeting in the middle, in agreement, and understanding that their difference of opinion came from their different approaches. Carl was a comedy purist, and Sheldon was all about the story, all about how the show was built.

I received a first-class education in comedy from listening to these two brilliant men argue with each other not about whether something *was* funny, but about what *constituted* funny, and what *made* something funny.

I listened to such discussions, but I stayed out of them, and avoided debates in general. My dislike of confrontation was so obvious that Rosie turned it into a joke. She dubbed me "the Six-Foot Tower of Jell-O," and anytime it seemed like someone needed to speak with Carl about a line, a scene, or some other issue, she turned to me and said, "Let's send the Six-Foot Tower of Jell-O."

From the get-go, we cracked each other up all the time. It was part of the process, and out of all of us, Richard Deacon, who played Alan Brady's brother-in-law Mel Cooley, was the worst at keeping it in. He started in the very first episode when he asked Rob if the writing staff could show him a little respect and Morey quips, "A *little* respect is all we're trying to show you." It was just zing—funny on the page and even funnier when we performed it.

And when Richard started to crack up, he got a quietly determined but panicked look in his eyes, and a single tiny bead of perspiration popped out on his forehead, which destroyed me. I always lost it before he did, then suffered the mirthful wrath of director John Rich yelling, "Cut." That was par for the course. Two seasons later, Joan Shawlee came on to play Morey's wife, Pickles, and little Larry Mathews, who played our son, Ritchie, kept saying, "Hi, Aunt Wrinkles." And that stopped the show.

Likewise, on one of the later episodes that season, I was supposed to toss my hat onto the hat rack in my office. All week long during rehearsals, and even during the run-through on the day we filmed, I flipped my fedora toward the peg and missed. Usually I missed badly. But when we got in front of the audience Tuesday night, I tossed my hat and it went straight onto the peg, and I mean straight, as if it were on a string. I looked genuinely surprised, which I was and which was okay—it still worked in the scene—and Rosie gave me a look that said, *Not bad,* which also worked as a beautifully underplayed moment that got a laugh on its own. But Morey ruined it. He couldn't hold back his astonishment.

"Holy shit!" he said to the audience. "He's been trying to do that all week."

P art of the fun of that first season was getting to know everyone. I was the new kid in town, so my eyes were wide open, and everyone had a full life going on outside of work. Rosie had been a performer since childhood, when she was a cute singer known as Baby Rose Marie, and she was a warmhearted New Yorker whose husband, Bobby Guy, the lead trumpet player in the NBC Orchestra, went through a mysterious illness that eventually took his life. She never lost the twinkle in her eyes, but it was hard on her.

Richard, who also played Lumpy Rutherford's father, Fred, on *Leave It to Beaver,* was a gourmet cook and connoisseur of fine things. He enjoyed laughing at himself and often noted that the best acting advice he ever got came from Helen Hayes at the start of his career when she told him to give up any thoughts of becoming a leading man.

Richard and Morey were unlikely best pals, but they were, and they frequently went out for drinks after work and came up with some of the best one-liners, insults, and bad jokes. That was Morey's specialty, coming up with those spot-on, hilarious insults.

Morey was a fascinating character with a joke for every person, situation, moment, or occasion. He claimed to know a hundred thousand jokes. But he had another side that few saw—or heard. The son of immigrants, he was a skilled musician who'd done stand-up with his brother in vaudeville and, as a teenager, worked in Al Capone's Chicago speakeasy. He wrote a couple of well-known songs in the 1940s, including "Rum and Coca-Cola." Few people know he also wrote lyrics to the show's theme song.

> *So you think that you got trouble*
> *Well, trouble's a bubble*
> *So tell old Mister Trouble to get lost.*

Why not hold your head up high, and
Stop cryin'
Start tryin'
And don't forget to keep your fingers crossed.

When you find the joy of livin'
Is lovin'
And givin'
You'll be there when the winning dice are tossed.

A smile's just a frown
That's turned upside down
So smile, and that frown
Will defrost
And don't forget to keep your fingers crossed.

I don't think anyone outside the show ever heard those lyrics until I began performing them with my singing group around 2004. Once you hear them arranged with the theme song, they put a smile on your face.

Morey was like that, too. He was a devoted husband and father of two children, and above all else a very happy man. He used to say he was the happiest person he knew. He was probably right.

On the set, Morey was usually on the phone with his broker or reading the business section of the paper and then talking to his broker. It was as if he ran a second business. During rehearsals, someone was always paging him, "Morey, we're ready for you. We're waiting."

It turned out the human joke machine was a financial genius. If not a genius, he had the magic touch when it came to picking stocks. He had bought a couple of winners early on, maybe Bethlehem Steel and Polaroid, and made a mint. I think he was richer than all the rest of us combined.

Mary was a hard worker who was going through a divorce from a man she had married at eighteen and was now falling in love with Grant Tinker, a former advertising executive turned TV producer who was frequently on the set with her. Mary kept her personal life quiet. She was a load of fun, though. Before we shot the pilot, Carl jokingly (I *think* he was joking) suggested that she and I go away for the weekend and get to know each other. We didn't. Once the show began airing, though, our chemistry was such that people actually thought we were husband and wife in real life.

When she was about seven or eight months pregnant, my wife came to the studio and watched a show being filmed. Afterward, she came backstage and said it didn't look like I was acting at all.

"You're exactly like you are at home," she said.

She was right, and that was all due to Carl's ability to render me perfectly on the page. I was pretty much the same person on and off the set—maybe to a fault. Early on, Sheldon gave me the only acting lesson I ever had when he came up to me after a taping, put his hands on my shoulders, and told me that I was doing a terrific job except for one small thing. It was my voice. He said that I spoke the same in every scene, in a monotone.

"Exaggerate a little," he said. "Let the audience *hear* your reaction."

"Okay," I said.

"Don't do much," he said. "Just raise and lower your voice."

I did. It worked. Simple.

11

CANCELED

That fall was a wonderful time in our lives, with a new show and the kids starting new schools, making new friends, trying to comprehend that they were still able to play in the swimming pool in October, and then, miraculously, saying hello to their new baby sister. It was four in the morning when Margie shook me awake and said, "It's time."

Only a moment passed before I realized she wasn't referring to the clock on the nightstand. No, she meant that after nearly nine months of watching her tummy grow, it was time to go to the hospital and meet the newest addition to our family. She was ready to have the baby.

The birth was like clockwork. Within thirty minutes, we were at St. John's Hospital in Santa Monica, and though it was the same place where we'd had an unpleasant experience a decade earlier, this time the only tears we shared were from the joy of welcoming our second daughter, Carrie Beth. She arrived with a smile on her face and wisps of blond hair on top of her pinkish head. Later, I handed out cigars to everyone on the set.

As Morey shook my hand, he exclaimed, "Wow, four kids with just one wife?"

That day, the *L.A. Times*' TV critic Cecil Smith was following me around for a story. We were working on the sixteenth episode of the season, "The Curious Thing About Women," which had Rob getting annoyed at Laura for opening his mail. During a break, I took a phone call from my agent and learned that I'd been asked to host the CBS Christmas showing of *The Wizard of Oz*. They wanted me to include my children, Chris, eleven, Barry, ten, and Stacy, six. I told my agent about our newest addition and he said, "She's included, too."

It gave Cecil a great anecdote for his story. After hanging up, I turned to everyone and said, "How about that? Three hours old and she's already in demand." In all seriousness, though, I thought she was too young to appear on TV. Morey immediately claimed injustice.

"Who's her agent?" Rosie asked.

"Never mind her agent," Morey said. "Who's her lawyer?"

Even when I tried to be serious, I failed. I used to say that I was getting paid to play. I often went into the set on Saturdays to work out little bits. I couldn't turn my brain off, that's how much fun I was having on the show. Take the episode "Where Did I Come From." One of my favorites, it opens with six-year-old Ritchie looking through his baby album while Laura and Rob sit on the sofa. After commenting on a photo, he asks where he came from.

Mary and I, as Laura and Rob, exchange one of those frightened looks that is familiar to parents caught off guard.

"Wha-wha-what did you say, Ritchie?" Rob stammers.

He repeats the question and Rob says there's not enough time to explain such a complicated thing. Then he turns to Laura and asks when *she* will have time to explain it to Ritchie. Unwilling to let her husband off the hook, she says there is still a half hour before bedtime, which sends Rob scrambling for Dr. Spock's child-rearing book. Something akin to that moment had actually happened to me at home, where Dr. Spock was our top and only authority. Our copy of his book was dog-eared in a hundred places.

"Rich, where do *you* think you came from?" Rob asks.

"Same place that Grandpa Helper came from," he says. "New Jersey."

Realizing Ritchie is not ready for Dr. Spock, and in fact isn't ready for the kind of specifics he feared, Rob says, "You didn't come from New Jersey. You come from New York. Don't you remember that?"

That line helps send the rest of the show into a wonderful series of flashbacks and reminiscences about the twenty-four hours leading up to Ritchie's birth. It was all about being a nervous husband, something I had recently gone through with Carrie Beth's birth, by the way, and something that came naturally to me. The show developed during rehearsals, where we all took a simple idea and kept adding to it until it was jam-packed with the most delicious comedy bits.

After this whirlwind, it concludes with Ritchie asking his mom if she liked that story. She nods yes.

"Better than *Black Beauty*?" he asks.

"Yes, better than *Black Beauty*," she agrees.

✦

In November, about a month after Carrie Beth was born, we had our own hell's a poppin'—or rather, hell's a burnin'—adventure: the Bel Air fire.

One day Margie looked up from the front yard and all of a sudden she called me to come see, to hurry and confirm the mind-boggling sight of flames shooting up across the horizon. If devils wore top hats, we were seeing the tips of them dancing up and down behind the not-too-distant mountains.

Within no time, the flames began to march over the hill and we had to evacuate. Police cars drove up the street, ordering residents to leave. We packed up quickly and I took the whole family to the studio. At night, we checked into a motel and stayed there for a couple of days.

The fire burned some houses along our street but skipped ours. During the next rain, though, the hillside above us slid down into our pool. I needed to have the entire hillside replanted and reinforced.

For about a week, all any of us talked about at work was the fire. It prompted everyone on the cast to talk about various disasters they had been in throughout their lives, which let Morey tell about a thousand new jokes on marriage. I talked about some of my days in the service, my various car problems, and of course the numerous tornado warnings I had experienced growing up in the Midwest, which also led me to share some stories about my younger brother, Jerry.

"The hardest I've ever laughed," I told people, "was one time when Jerry and I had jobs as surveyors."

"A summer job?" someone asked.

"No, it was winter," I explained. "I was seventeen, and Jerry was twelve. We were out in a field. There was snow up to our knees. And it was freezing cold—below freezing, actually. We were trying to take measurements and he said something funny and we started to laugh. Except our faces were frozen stiff. We couldn't laugh. We could see it beneath the surface, but we couldn't get it out. If you look at someone who's trying to laugh but can't, it's even funnier. As we stared at each other, we laughed even harder. We were dying."

My brother, who had been funny his whole life, had gotten into show business, too. He and my parents had driven out to California (and camped the whole way) when I was doing the Merry Mutes act. They saw Phil and me perform at the Georgian Hotel in Santa Monica. Impressed that I was making a living—such as it was—lip-syncing to records, Jerry went home, got himself a partner, and started doing our act, pantomiming to songs.

When he went into the Air Force, Jerry got into Tops in Blue, a comedy-variety show that traveled from base to base. He swiped material from Dick Shawn's act, including a piece called "Massa Richard," which he performed better than Dick. He also incorporated jokes from other comics. In those days, no one could check.

Gradually, he included his own material. When I first saw him, I thought, My God, he's got the timing! If you don't have that talent, you can't do stand-up. But my brother had it, and he began working some of the Playboy clubs, which put him on the map. Dan Rowan and Dick Martin took him on the road with them. Later he opened for Steve Lawrence and Eydie Gorme.

He had just turned thirty the summer I began doing *The Dick Van Dyke Show,* and Carl heard me tell stories about Jerry's antics, from punching the high-school dean to his skill playing the four-string banjo.

One day after the Bel Air fire, a bunch of us were telling stories around the table and I mentioned that my brother had been a longtime sleepwalker. It had lasted until he was in his late teens.

"He'd just get up out of bed and leave," I said, getting up from the table myself and acting out the way Jerry used to walk through the house as he slept. "We had to go get him one night. Some people called from across town. He had walked there in his pajamas."

Rosie, Morey, and the others were incredulous.

"One night I caught him going out the door with our dad's golf clubs," I said. "He had the bag over his shoulder. I asked where he was going and he said, 'To play golf.' "

"Did he know what he was doing?" Carl asked.

"Yes, that was the strange thing," I said. "Growing up, we slept in the same bedroom, and I'd say, 'Jerry.' He'd say, 'I know. I'm asleep. Just give me a few minutes.' Then he continued walking around the house. He almost got thrown out of the Air Force because he still walked in his sleep."

Carl, who was always listening to, adapting, and incorporating our real-life stories into the show, caught Jerry's act in Las Vegas, thought he was as funny as I had said, and wrote a two-part episode based on the stories I'd told about Jerry being a sleepwalker and nearly getting thrown out of the service because of it. Once again, Carl amazed me with his finely tuned ear and creativity.

Jerry was excited about being on a network show. It was a break for him, and he hoped it might lead to something else, something bigger, as did I. He did gain more recognition, and we had a good time working together, the first time we'd done so on camera.

By the time the two-parter aired at the end of March 1962, though, it seemed as if there might not be another chance. Worse, it appeared that I would have to go looking for another job myself.

CBS canceled the show. Sheldon delivered the news on the set. It was a ratings issue, he explained. Despite good reviews and a whole season of thirty-nine episodes to prove ourselves, we lost the ratings war each week to our more popular time-slot competition, *The Perry Como Show*. In short, we didn't find an audience.

"Or they didn't find us," someone said, voicing a frequent complaint that we didn't receive enough promotion from the network.

As the Six-Foot Tower of Jell-O, I didn't see the point in complaining. The facts were the facts, and the network had made its decision. I felt sick. The whole lot of us was practically suicidal. We knew we had something good and we didn't want it to end prematurely. I glanced around the set. It felt like a foreclosure, like we were being wrongly booted from our home. It seemed like such a tragic error in judgment.

The show aside, I was personally devastated. We had just moved across country, bought a house, and had a fourth child. I had recently signed on to do the movie version of *Bye Bye Birdie*. My salary would hold us for about a year. But then what?

12

BUSINESS AS USUAL

I t was spring on the bustling studio's back lot, and I was
involved in a rehearsal of the big Conrad Birdie number
when my limbs suddenly stiffened. My knees locked and my
feet hesitated when normally they flew on automatic pilot. The
problem was temporary, though. After a moment, I regained my
rhythm and my arms and legs returned to their rubbery precision.
The reason for the freeze? Fred Astaire.

Out of the corner of my eye, I caught the legendary dancer
watching the run-through. He was in the back, concealed in the
gray shadows beyond the lights, but he was unmistakable.

As soon as we took a break, he walked up to me and said
hello. Not only did he remind me that we had met in New York,
but he also flattered me by saying he was a fan of *The Dick Van
Dyke Show*. Then he went on to explain that he'd come to the
set hoping to see me dance. He loved the way I moved. There

was only one thing I could possibly say in response, and that was "thank you."

What else was I going to say?

"Thank you, and I like the way you move, too."

No, such compliments are rare, and I treasured this one. I still do. Someone had a camera and we posed together—the legend and the luckiest guy on the lot, I thought. I was wearing a nicely tailored suit, but I looked like a tramp next to Fred Astaire. He had that impeccable, iconic sense of style. It was part of that special thing that made him unique.

My dad had been the same in his own way. He wasn't as suave as Fred. I mean, who was? But my dad had a taste for nice clothes and an eye for small, stylish touches. In fact, as I chatted with Fred, I thought of my dad, who had always liked nice suits and for a brief time even wore a silk tie around his waist instead of a belt because he had seen Fred Astaire do it.

Fred asked if I was enjoying myself on the film. I said I was, explaining that it was my first and quite exciting and I was learning a lot. I missed working with Chita, who had been passed over by the movie's producers, but I was partnered in her place with Janet Leigh, who was not only an Oscar-nominated movie star but a real doll, lots of fun on and off camera, and a warm, generous woman who had my entire family over to her house many times.

All of us adored her.

She wasn't much of a dancer, though you wouldn't have known from the way choreographer Anna White worked with her individually and the two of us together. A Broadway veteran, White figured out our capabilities and made sure we looked good. But Janet's limitations in that area might have diminished her standing with the film's director, George Sidney, who was, quite obviously, enamored with the movie's young star, Ann-Margret.

Then again, even if Janet had moved like Ginger Rogers, it's likely that Sidney would still have been fixated on the very talented redhead. What wasn't to like about her? She was talented and sexy and just exuded the kind of energy and charisma that let you know a major star was being born.

But Sidney's embrace of that potential made the film very different from the play. One afternoon, Janet and I walked onto the set after lunch. She was carping that she wasn't getting as much screen time as she had been led to believe before shooting began. She didn't know that for sure, I said. None of us had seen any of the dailies.

Then we stepped inside the soundstage and I stopped.

"Uh-oh," I said.

"What?" Janet asked.

I motioned toward the stage. Ann-Margret was sitting on George Sidney's lap.

"I think we're in trouble," I said.

"Oh yeah."

Nothing was going on other than the director was smitten with a young woman who was about to have the same effect on countless moviegoers. *C'est la vie,* especially in Hollywood. You couldn't say a bad word about Ann-Margret. Sweet and polite and barely out of her teens, she was an extremely shy young woman until it was time to work. Then she lit up. She strove to do everything perfectly.

For the most part, though, she kept to herself. In rehearsals, I had a habit of clowning around and enjoying myself. She didn't like that. She was very serious, very focused.

The opposite was true of Paul Lynde, the only actor other than me from the original Broadway production to reprise his role in the movie. Of course, as far as I was concerned, he was irreplaceable. I'm glad the producers felt the same way. And then there was Maureen Stapleton, not to be confused with the television star Jean Stapleton.

Maureen, cast as my mother despite being only six months older than I was, was an immensely talented actress who'd won a Tony Award in 1951 for starring in Tennessee Williams's play *The Rose Tattoo*. But she was a bigger and more memorable character in real life than any she played onstage or in film. Brash and bawdy, she was quite open about having gotten into the business in the 1940s because of her lust for actor Joel McCrea. She was quite open about many of her urges.

She also had more phobias than any human being I had ever met in my life. She had never been on an airplane. She refused to get in an elevator. And when we left the studio for lunch, I had to hold her hand as we crossed Sunset Boulevard. She was too nervous to cross by herself.

Maureen walked around the set with a little paper sack. A little nip here and there kept her calm, though her calm occasionally turned quite boisterous and bawdy, depending on the amount she nipped. When the movie wrapped, George Sidney hosted a party at his house, a formal mansion in Beverly Hills. A butler greeted guests and servers and staff bustled inside and out. This was the first Hollywood party I had ever been to, and I was impressed. I half expected to run into royalty.

Instead, I ran into Maureen and Paul, who arrived together. They were already sloshed. Paul couldn't face people unless he'd had a couple of drinks, and Maureen was hanging on to him, wearing a muumuu and pearls. Both looked like they were swaying in a strong wind—except there was nary a breeze. I lost them during the cocktail hour, but dinner starred Paul.

All of us sat at a long table in the dining room. After George

Sidney thanked everyone for their contributions to the film, Paul leaned in holding his wineglass as if he were going to say something similar. He didn't. He held on to the quiet until anticipation built, then he looked at the picture's star.

"Ann-Margret," he said, "I just want you to know that I'm the only one at this table who doesn't want to screw you."

George Sidney's elderly and quite proper mother gasped. If this had been a movie, something would've popped out of her mouth for comedic effect. It was one of those unbelievably audacious moments that momentarily stops time. But it didn't stop Paul. He couldn't have cared less. This was his milieu. You could almost see the sparkle in his one-hundred-proof eyes as the wickedly funny one-liners lined up like cars waiting to go through a tollbooth.

Maureen toasted each one of his off-color remarks until she was quite toasted herself. It was out of control, and it didn't get any less astonishing when we adjourned to the living room for after-dinner drinks. Maureen was still on her salad, which she carried with her and ate with toothpicks while sitting and sometimes half lying on the floor.

We all tried to act as if there wasn't an elephant in the room. But that lasted only so long.

"Maureen," I finally said, "wouldn't you like to sit in a chair?"

"I'd tell you where I'd like to sit," she said. "But your wife is here."

I didn't know how to respond. But I didn't have to. A few minutes later, the maid suffered a heart attack. Paramedics arrived and treated her there on the living room floor where we'd been partying. By the time they took her to the hospital, Maureen was stark naked in the swimming pool, flailing around and calling for the rest of us to join her.

On the drive home, Margie and I laughed hysterically as we recounted all of the wild shenanigans. I wondered if all Hollywood parties were like that. Of course, they weren't, and the movie's actual premiere in early 1963 paled in comparison. Almost anything would.

For the premiere, though, Margie and I and Janet and her husband, Robert Brandt, hired a car to take us to the screening in Santa Barbara. We wanted to make it a fun night. But after the movie, Janet was livid. She had no idea that Ann-Margret's part was going to be so all-consuming and hers would be so minor. After production was completed, Sidney had filmed an additional opening and closing number with Ann-Margret. We saw it for the first time there.

In the lobby, Janet cornered the director and said, "Where the hell did that song come from?"

It wasn't the movie she'd signed on for, and as far as I was concerned, it wasn't the play. But as they say, that's showbiz.

By then, CBS had changed its mind about *The Dick Van Dyke Show* and we were well into the second season. I was still working on *Birdie* when the decision was made. Sheldon had gone directly to the sponsor, Procter & Gamble, and persuaded them to stick with us. However, an even more persuasive argument came from the viewers.

It turned out the show found an audience during summer reruns, and vice versa—the audience found the show. They embraced it, in fact. Without competition from Perry Como, ratings soared. When the second season began in September 1962, with the Petrie family mourning the death of one of Ritchie's two pet ducks, an episode called "Never Name a Duck," the show cracked TV's Top 10. From there, we never looked back.

A funny thing happened that second season when Mary and I went back to work. We couldn't stop giggling when we were around each other. Part of it was the joy of being back together with everyone and getting to continue the series, but our giggles continued past the first episode or two. I finally asked a psychiatrist friend of mine about it. He stated what was patently obvious.

"Dick, you've got a crush on her."

I put my head in my hands and laughed.

Of course I did.

Who didn't adore Mary?

If we had been different people, maybe something would have happened. But neither of us was that type of person.

Still, we were stuck on each other.

And others were stuck on us. In addition to ratings, Carl won an Emmy for his writing achievements during the first season, and John Rich received a well-deserved nomination for directing. Both men had done a remarkable job, writing and directing almost every one of the thirty-nine episodes that year. It's something that still stands out, perhaps even more so because for some shows nowadays an entire season might be comprised of only six or eight episodes. Prolificacy aside, the shows were home runs.

For season two, they were back at it. Carl continued to draw on all of our lives for material. In the episode "A Bird in the Head Hurts," Ritchie is traumatized after a woodpecker pecks him in the head. Well, that had actually happened to Carl's son, Rob. Likewise, Carl's determination to pick up the check every time we went out to lunch or dinner inspired the episode "My Husband Is a Check-Grabber." And when he wrote "The Cat Burglar" episode about a phantom burglar who breaks into the Petries' home, he basically retold an embarrassing story I had recounted to him about an incident that happened to Margie and me when we lived on Long Island.

In the show, Rob and Laura hear a noise at night and think a cat burglar who has been working the neighborhood has targeted their house. Rob gets out a tiny semiautomatic, but his bullets are in a jewelry case with a ballerina on top. Every time he tries to open it to get the ammo, it plays "The Blue Danube." In real life, Margie and I heard a loud noise outside and were convinced someone was trying to break into our home.

I was petrified except for the fact that I had, after much debate, recently bought a small .22 rifle. Moving quietly, I got the gun out of hiding and prepared to defend my family. A moment later, though, I turned to my wife with a look of horror on my face.

"What's wrong?" she said in a whisper.

I thought even that was too much noise and put my finger to my mouth, telling her to shush. I tried to respond without making a sound.

"I don't know what you're saying," she whispered.

I tried again.

"I can't see to read your lips," she said. "It's too dark."

"I can't find the bullets," I said.

"Oh," she said, rolling her eyes as if I should have known. "They're in my jewelry box."

I tiptoed across the room to her dresser and opened the jewelry box. As soon as I lifted the lid, it started to play music, "The Blue Danube." I slammed it shut and gave her a look. Why had she put the bullets in her jewelry box? How was I going to get them out without the burglar hearing Johann Strauss's famous waltz? What was I going to do?

I stood there, waiting for something to happen, and when nothing did, I picked up my unloaded rifle, pretended it was in fact ready for business, and went to see what was what. In the end, I didn't find anything out of the ordinary. Margie and I were sure we had heard a noise outside, but the rest must have been our imaginations running scared.

M y father had a difficult time reconciling my success. "Never in my wildest imagination," he used to say. I was on the phone with him one Saturday, telling him about everything that was happening to me, and his amazement nearly matched mine. He made a surprising confession: He never thought I would amount to much of anything.

"Do you remember the summer you sold shoes in my brother's store?" he asked.

"Yeah, sure," I said. "I was paid on commission."

"How many shoes did you sell?" he asked.

"I don't remember exactly," I said. "But pretty close to none."

"Son, I have to tell you, I feared everything you touched was going to work out like that," he said, laughing. "Your grandmother is here and we're all proud of what you're doing."

Having given up his life as a bon vivant jazz musician and baseball player when I came along, my father not only marveled that I was making a living from my passion for having fun, but he also appreciated it as much as I did. I had a five-picture deal with Columbia, and I had a separate production company with my manager, Byron, who was negotiating for several projects, including one with my idol Stan Laurel for a film on Laurel and Hardy.

I also had a two-album recording deal, an invitation to headline at the Sahara Hotel in Las Vegas, and as soon as the second season of *The Dick Van Dyke Show* wrapped I began work on the movie *What a Way to Go*.

The comedy, written by the multitalented Broadway legend Betty Comden, told the story of a wealthy woman marrying one man after another, and getting wealthier with each one, all of whom happened to die prematurely as they struggled to make more and more money. Shirley MacLaine starred along with Paul Newman, Robert Mitchum, Dean Martin, Robert Cummings, and me, in the role of her first husband, meaning I had a small part and died early.

But I had fun. Shirley was a rascal. We were on location one day and she didn't want her makeup man to touch her up, so she took off across a field, running at full speed. I watched in puzzled amusement as her makeup man sprinted after her, caught up, and tackled her as if they were two football players in the open field. Pinning her down, he applied makeup. Both of them returned to the set laughing.

Before I departed, I had one scene with Dean Martin, an easygoing, friendly man who referred to me as Dickie. Anybody from the nightclub circuit, especially comics, has a diminutive name like Dean-o, Jackie, Billy, Sammy, or in my case, Dickie. Dean played a guy who stole Shirley from me. His dad owned the big department store in town. As we worked, I thought, There is no way they can use this footage. The man is smashed.

True to form, Dean had been drinking on the set while entertaining various beautiful women who had come to visit him. One day it was Ursula Andress, the next day it was some other babe.

He seemed to treat every hour as if it were happy hour. But when I saw him on screen, I couldn't tell he was drunk—and neither could anyone else. He was just Dean being Dean. That's what he did, and it obviously worked for him.

After making the movie, I found myself thinking about what worked for me, and also what I wanted to do for work, what was important to me, and what I wanted my work to say about me.

13

A JOLLY HOLIDAY

Following *What a Way to Go*, I determined to be more careful about the choices I made. The movie's script had been a pleasure to read, but the final version included some colorful ad-libbing that made it significantly different, more adult in tone, and had I known that initially I would have turned it down.

I met my agent, Sol Leon, for lunch at the commissary, and talked through my concerns. He asked the obvious questions: What kind of films did I want to make? Where did I see myself going in terms of movies? What sort of scripts should he look for?

"I've thought about this," I said, "and I'm pretty clear on it. I only want to make movies that my children can see."

"Only kids' movies?" he asked.

"Not kids' movies," I clarified. "I want to make movies that I can see with my kids and not feel uncomfortable."

He expressed slight worry that that might limit my opportunities, particularly at this time when standards in Hollywood, like the culture itself, were beginning to change and evolve into what we remember as the more liberal, experimental Sixties. But I didn't share his worries. I had a long-term vision in mind. One of an actor's biggest challenges, perhaps his or her most important, is choosing the right role. I knew that having a well-defined standard would ultimately help my representatives find the right material, and if they did their jobs right, and I did mine, ultimately the material would define me in a way that would make me comfortable for the rest of my career.

It was similar to Carl wanting *The Dick Van Dyke Show* to be timeless, or Fred Astaire movies seeming classic. If I always felt comfortable taking the whole family to one of my films, I knew others would, too, and that would serve me well over time.

I could play many types of characters on camera, but all were, in some way, going to be variations of me, and I was conscious of who I was. I wasn't a prude or a goody two-shoes, but I was, in many ways, still the boy my mother praised for being good, and though older and more complex, I was content with remaining that good boy.

I wanted to be able to talk about my work at the dinner table and hold my head up on Sundays when my wife and I led our children into the Brentwood Presbyterian Church, where I was an elder. I did have a wild side, and I showed it every time I walked through the front door and my littlest child, Carrie Beth, made me dance to Herb Alpert and the Tijuana Brass's hit song "Tijuana Sauerkraut." But you were not going to see me acting up at Hollywood parties. For the most part, you weren't going to see me *at* any Hollywood parties. I stayed home. That kind of family-oriented, value-driven ethos earned the admiration of another Midwesterner, the Chicago-born Walt Disney.

The visionary studio owner and entrepreneur who had created Mickey Mouse, won an Oscar for *Snow White,* overseen classics and favorites from *Pinocchio* and *Fantasia* to *The Absent-Minded Professor* and *The Parent Trap,* as well as opened Disneyland, had read an interview in which I stated my intention to stick to family movies. He liked that. He thought it made me perfect for his type of Disney movies—and specifically for the one he was about to start working on, *Mary Poppins.*

As a result of the interest he took in me, I was offered the role of Bert the chimney sweep, opposite Julie Andrews, who had been cast as the practically perfect nanny Mary Poppins. It was my dream to be in a Disney picture, and I knew from the outset that this project, based on the beloved P. L. Travers books, was no ordinary one.

There have only been two times in my career when I have known that I had a chance to be involved in something special. The first was *The Dick Van Dyke Show,* and the second was when I read the script for *Poppins.* I will never forget putting it down, turning to Margie, and telling her that it was sensational.

It got even better after I signed my contract and met Walt at his studio in Burbank. He impressed me as a nice man, really an old shoe. I later heard that he was a tough taskmaster, but I only saw his easygoing side, the side that led others to refer to him as Uncle Walt.

We talked in his office, and I learned that he had pursued the rights to making this book into a film for nearly twenty-five years. He took me down the hall and into room after room, where he showed me storyboards for the movie. Gorgeous renderings, they hung on the walls like paintings in a museum. He went over each one, pointing out details, talking about the sets that were being built, mentioning that work on the songs and script had been going on for two years, and savoring the picture he already saw in his head.

"What do you think?" he asked at one point.

"I'm speechless," I said.

"I have more to show you," he said, smiling.

He introduced me to several of the animators, all of whom were of varying ages but with one thing in common: No matter their age, they were all kids. None had ever lost the child inside him. I related easily to them. And admired their talent. Next, Walt took me to meet a wonderful guy who managed all of the sound effects for the studio. He had a huge room with a number of different machines, many, if not all of them, he had invented. Finally, Walt took me to meet the Sherman brothers. That was the icing on an already delicious cake.

In their mid-thirties, Richard and Robert Sherman were staff writers at Disney who had been hired personally by Walt. They shook my hand warmly and chatted with Walt about work, before Walt asked them to play me some songs. Richard, the more out-going of the two, sat at the piano while Robert took a seat across the room, after which he shot a quick glance at his brother.

"Walt, should I play your favorite?" Richard asked.

"Not yet," he said. "Save it for last."

"All right," said Richard, who, with a puckish smile, dove into the instantly fun and contagious "Supercalifragilisticexpialido-cious," and then followed that with "Chim Chim Cher-ee," "Let's Go Fly a Kite," and several songs intended for Julie, including "A Spoonful of Sugar." He might have been finished at that point, except that Walt gave him a nod, which Richard knew meant that the boss wanted to hear his favorite, "Feed the Birds."

When he finally looked up, finished with his bravura per-formance for this privileged audience of two, Walt and myself, I clapped. I wanted to say something along the lines of "That was spectacular," but the music had left me speechless. Imagine hearing those songs, now such an established part of the movie musical lexicon, for the first time. It was a stunning experience.

With some, I tried to sing along. Others put a smile on my face, as they did on Walt's, and also filled me with excitement and anticipation of performing them. Those songs didn't just get under my skin, they became a part of me then and there, and thinking about it now, they've never left.

Later at home, Margie asked how it had gone at the studio.

"It was pretty special," I said. "I think we've got a real movie here."

D ance rehearsals were the hardest part of *Poppins*. We practiced on Disney's back lot for six weeks if not longer during a heat wave that would have made the Mojave feel cool. Before we started, Walt asked if I knew any good choreographers. I was surprised he did not know any himself. I recommended Marc Breaux and Dee Dee Wood, a young couple with whom I had worked on an Andy Williams special. As I told Walt, they had impressed me as very inventive—and he hired them.

They did a heck of a job on the picture. And for me, they were perfect. That may have been Walt's genius in asking me. Who knows. But Marc and Dee Dee made me stretch and do things I hadn't done before. Nearly forty, I worked with dancers at least ten years younger than I was, but I stayed with them and they were all fun and supportive. One of the most challenging yet purely fun numbers for me was the dance with the penguins. It was all mime and dance, which I loved to do, but it was done against a green screen on an empty set, and we did take after take because every move I made had to be perfect since the penguins and backdrop were painted in later.

I had the perfect partner in Julie Andrews. She had her baby daughter, Emma, with her when we met, so my first impressions were of her warmth and tenderness as a mother. As time went on, her prodigious talent unfolded along with a delightful personality. I saw why she had been cast in the role of the "practically perfect" nanny.

She was a lady first and foremost, but she also had a great, whimsical sense of humor. I never once saw her get angry about anything or utter a single complaint. Before agreeing to do the film, she had balked at the romantic ballad, "The Eyes of Love," asking Walt to replace it with something else, and the Sherman brothers came back with "A Spoonful of Sugar," perhaps one of the all-time great fixes. Only one thing surpassed Julie's spot-on instincts, and that was her voice.

We were still in the early stages of production when we recorded the score, and it scared me to death because Julie's voice could have been used to tune a piano. She was pitch perfect—and I never was. I was enjoyably close. As such, recording with her was a challenge.

But even the hard stuff felt right. The Sherman brothers were in the studio with us, and always pleasant. Walt was a frequent visitor on the set, but he wasn't one of those executives who was really a frustrated director and came around only to inject his whims and ideas, even with this project, which had been such a longtime passion of his. He seemed pleased with what he saw.

Director Robert Stevenson had, in many respects, the easiest job. He was fairly mechanical and didn't do much directing other than to say, "Perfect. Let's do another one just like that." In my opinion, the movie's unsung hero was the online producer and co-writer, Bill Walsh, a heavyset man with the most wonderful sense of humor.

As with any great film, there's always someone responsible for the spirit the audience experiences, and as far as I'm concerned, Bill created the lighthearted atmosphere that let all of us forget that we were working and instead feel like we were floating a few feet off the ground through a Hollywood playground, as if we had embarked on a jolly holiday.

Speaking of such, the charming song "Jolly Holiday" was more demanding than Mary and Bert's little stroll through the countryside appears. It was shot against a green screen (the lush background was painted in later), but every minute spent staring into that bright yellow sulfur light was worth it because I still smile when I think of Bert floating gently above the ground (as he sings, "I feel like I could fly") and Mary, after gently pulling him back to Earth, scolding, "Now, Bert, none of your larking about."

Such fun!

Ironically, the song "I Love to Laugh," which I do, was even harder than any of us expected. It's the scene where Bert summons Mary to help with her uncle Albert, played by the great Ed Wynn, who has a case of the laughs, which causes him to soar high above the ground. Mary arrives with the Banks children, Jane and Michael, and soon everyone catches not spots but the giggles and ends up having tea up by the ceiling.

Again, this was a gloriously fun number to perform, and built around a clever idea, but my diaphragm ached from laughing all day. I wondered if it was even possible to hurt your diaphragm from too much laughing. I guessed so. There was also a lot of hanging around in the air on high wires as lights were adjusted, cameras changed, and retakes done while we were supposed to be floating high above the floor.

A couple times we broke for lunch and the crew started to leave, forgetting Julie, the kids, Ed, and I were all strapped into wires and hanging thirty feet above the ground. I yelled, "Guys, don't forget about us!"

Poor Ed, who was in the high eighties and not well, was absolutely wonderful and worth the price of admission just to see him going through various acrobatics while suffering belly laughs that all of us caught. There were no such dangers when we performed "Chim Chim Cher-ee," Bert's moody ode to the lucky life of a chimney sweep, a remarkable number on many levels for what it conveys.

Then it goes into that mesmerizing dance across the roofs of London, which was and remains great fun to watch, but oh boy, it was strenuous to do. We shot numerous takes. I went home those days and just dropped. The song "Step in Time," inspired by an old English bar song called "Knees up Mother Brown," was similarly exhausting.

Julie and I both loved performing "Supercalifragilisticexpialidocious." How could you feel otherwise? The Sherman brothers said that extraordinary word stemmed from their plays with double-talk. It also had the catchy bounce of an old English musical number. It made the kid in me smile the first time I heard it, and it has continued to make kids everywhere smile.

Oddly, I don't have anything to do with my favorite song in the movie, "The Perfect Nanny," which is the advertisement that the two Banks children, Jane (Karen Dotrice) and Michael (Matthew Garber), have composed and then sing to their mother and father, who are looking for a new nanny after the old one has taken flight. Something about their high-pitched English voices hit me every time, probably the same way that Walt got emotional every time he heard "Feed the Birds."

The music—as good music always does—opened the door in our souls to something deep and lasting. For Walt, it was sentimentalism. For me, it was childhood innocence.

We had been rehearsing the dance numbers for several weeks when I asked Walt if I could take on a second role, that of the elderly banker Mr. Dawes. I loved portraying old men, and since first reading the script, I had been secretly eyeing that part, which included the song "Fidelity Fiduciary Bank." I saw a lot of potential for extracurricular amusement.

So one day early in production I asked Walt for a moment of his time and made my pitch. I even offered to do the extra work for free.

He studied me with an expression that conveyed uncertainty—not what I expected.

"You'll have to test," he said finally.

Even though I had hoped to hear a different response, I was no less enthusiastic about the opportunity to have some additional fun. Just getting made up for the test as a balding old man in his nineties made my day, and by the time the last wisps of white hair and beard were added to my face I was stooped over, talking like the very senior banker, and having a blast amusing both the crew and myself. For the test itself, I stood in front of the Bankses' house and ad-libbed a few lines, excusing myself every few minutes to pee in the bushes.

"I'm a weak old man because of a hernia," I explained in a wheezy voice, and while uttering those words, I teetered on the edge of the curb as if it were a perilous drop down the face of a cliff. The crew ate it up.

So did Walt.

Not only did he agree to let me play the old banker, but he also found my teetering so amusing he ordered a six-inch-high step built inside the bank's door to let me reprise my gimmick. But Walt, on top of all his other attributes, was a shrewd horse trader, and he refused to simply indulge my desire to play this little part without getting a little something out of it.

He made it contingent on me donating four thousand dollars to the three-year-old art school he had founded, California Institute of the Arts. In other words, I ended up paying him a not insignificant amount of money to play a part I had offered to do for free. I still scratch my head at that one.

But it was worth every dollar. I would have, in fact, paid even more.

While we were in production, I knew the movie was special. All of us did. It was apparent from the start and more so through numerous test screenings. The movie finally opened at the end of August 1964 with a star-studded premiere at Grauman's Chinese Theatre in Hollywood. At the end, there was a standing ovation that filled the enormous theater, and later the *New York Times* would call it a "most wonderful, cheering movie" and "irresistible."

Certainly those at the premiere felt that way. At the after-party, silent-film star Francis X. Bushman took hold of my hand and said, "Sir, you are a national treasure." Maurice Chevalier introduced himself and said he wanted me to play him in a movie. Julie was similarly overwhelmed with praise. All of us were. As far as I recall, only one person had a contrary opinion, and that was the book's author, P. L. Travers. Apparently she approached Walt and said all of the animation should be removed. Walt was unfazed.

"Sorry," he said. "But the ship has already sailed."

Indeed, what a fine voyage, too.

14

FAMILY VALUES

Let's just say I was warned. I was guest starring on the Danny Kaye special as a way of promoting the third season of *The Dick Van Dyke Show,* and on the first day of rehearsal the director warned me that Danny had quit smoking five weeks earlier in preparation of working with me. I responded with a look that was easily read as "Really?"

"Yeah, he figured he better have his wind," the director said.

I smiled. Only later did it dawn on me that Danny might have felt challenged if not a little threatened by going toe to toe with me on his own show. The two of us had a big production number together, a musical sketch set in a courtroom where I played a disheveled old Clarence Darrow–type lawyer and Danny was a dapper hotshot attorney. But on day two of rehearsals, I returned to the studio and found out that our parts had been switched. No explanation was given until the later part of the afternoon when a producer took me aside and said that I'd gotten too many laughs as the old man.

Later, when I had my own specials, I approached them as opportunities to have fun with performers whom I admired. It was playtime for me, and hopefully the viewers at home would enjoy it as much as I did. But I understood what was going on with Danny. I didn't say anything. Then again, I didn't have to.

I responded in the only way I could, the only way that made sense. I became Nijinsky. I danced off the walls, leapt over tables and chairs, and afterward, when Danny shook my hand and said he'd enjoyed having me on the show, I offered an easygoing smile and said the feeling was mutual.

With *The Dick Van Dyke Show* an audience favorite and according to some critics carving out a niche in TV history, I was too consumed with our inspired brand of fun to let those kinds of situations bother me. I was also too busy. That season, Carl expanded the team with veteran comedy writers Bill Persky and Sam Denoff. Carl gave them the lowdown on the show's ethos and they contributed brilliantly on and off the page.

Sam was a character who spent the Friday run-through for the writers leaning back in his chair, with his head tilted back and his eyes closed, listening to us; then every once in a while, he would stop us in our tracks with a foghorn-like bellow, "Boring!" Bill was also an original, a smart man with a steady hand who could get a laugh just by raising his big, thick eyebrows but who kept the atmosphere light and interesting with jokes, impressions, and a wry take on just about every topic imaginable.

The best writers were philosophers who wrapped their com-mentary about life in laughter. Carl's other hires included Garry Marshall, the future creator of *Happy Days,* and Jerry Belson, both of whom went on to magnificent careers. Jerry Paris also began to direct. The show became its own little world, with its internal rhythm and high standards, and also a playground for talented performers on their way up, including Don Rickles, Jamie Farr, Greg Morris, Joan Shawlee, Herbie Faye, and Allan Melvin.

Being part of such a talented ensemble was my idea of heaven. We were so successful creating a feeling of family that many people thought Mary and I were really husband and wife, including some of those at the Emmy Awards the previous May, where, even though the attendees were from the industry, Mary and I were consoled as a married couple when we failed to win in our respective categories. Rosie also lost that year, while Carl, John Rich, and the show itself captured trophies.

For a smooth mover, as I was often called, I was less than suave when it came to handling individual stardom, which was never my thing. My favorite example of my awkwardness in such situations occurred one rainy morning on the freeway as I was on my way to work. Suddenly, in a burst of blue and gray smoke, my Jaguar seized up and sputtered to a stop. Oil had leaked out of the crankcase and the car was dead in the middle lane.

Although rush hour, I stepped out of the car—and that's when the real problems started. As I waved at cars to stop so I could push my Jag across the lanes to the side, people began to recognize me. Not only did cars stop, but a few got out and asked for autographs as well. A producer named Tom Naud appeared from out of nowhere and handed me a script, explaining that he had been trying to get it to me and wasn't this a lucky break.

For everyone but me. Two cops showed up to assist me and both turned out to be amateur dancers who couldn't wait to show me a few steps. A former vaudeville performer ran the garage where I was towed, and he dusted off his old act as I waited for one of his servicemen to examine the car. Despite hours of inconvenience, it turned out to be an interesting morning.

I n early 1964, we purchased a thirty-five-year-old California-style ranch home in Encino. The family home, with property that included a swimming pool and majestic old oak trees, satisfied my craving for normalcy. (I'd be remiss if I didn't mention how much the cat loved hiding out in the oak trees and then terrorizing our dogs by jumping down onto their backs.) I decorated my office with my first Emmy, which I won that May, and Margie continued doing a terrific job keeping the kids grounded and on track.

She had no fondness for show business. She appreciated Hollywood, but was not drawn to it. I knew events like the Emmys were hard on her. She was, as with many spouses, constantly shunted to the side by people wanting to chat with me or by reporters who stepped between us even if we were mid-conversation. She was earthy and artistic, with an array of interests. She wore her hair short and eschewed makeup. We were often mistaken as brother and sister since many people thought of me as being with Mary.

She came to tapings every so often but otherwise felt no need to go every week. As she frequently said with a laugh, I was pretty much the same there as I was at home. Once, when I was on the cover of a magazine, she went to the grocery store and bought six copies. The woman ringing her up at the counter said she must know someone in the magazine.

Margie said, yes, she did. "Dick Van Dyke."

"Isn't that wonderful." The woman grinned. "Are you his mother?"

So Margie's attitude to the glitz and glamour was a simple

"no, thank you." I wasn't much better. Among those in Hollywood, I was regarded as a square—a funny square, but a square nonetheless. I preferred to think of myself as grounded, sensible, and an everyman who hadn't lost touch with the small town, mid-American values that I'd learned in childhood.

I took pride when Mary told a reporter that I was "the nicest actor" she had ever met. "Even-tempered, considerate, almost saintlike." Hardly saintlike. In a story I wrote for U.P.I., I painted a pretty normal, if not boring, picture of myself, explaining that I "spent most of my spare time with my family. We don't go to big Hollywood parties, and we don't give them, either."

If that made me a square, so be it. "I take that as a compliment," I wrote.

I was concerned about doing a good job as a husband, father, and human being. As far as I was concerned, children learned right and wrong and how to behave more from watching their parents than from anything they were told, and I wanted to be a good role model at home. I spent weekends with the family. I surfed with the boys in Malibu. I played music and sang with the girls. I led family sing-alongs, and play-alongs for that matter, as everyone seemed to be involved in learning an instrument.

Every Sunday, we attended the Brentwood Presbyterian Church. I didn't teach Sunday school as I had in New York, but I spoke to the congregation on occasion. My brief interest in becoming a minister was far behind me, but I was intensely curious and even passionate about God. I had read and continued to read Buber, Tilich, Bonhoeffer, and Tournier, all theologians whom I thought helped explain religion in a practical, rational sense as far as everyday life as opposed to the strict doctrines of religion.

I was all about living a kind, righteous, moral, forgiving, and loving life seven days a week, not just the one day when you went to church. I thought about it quite a bit, noticed the differences in others, and I shared my opinions when the appropriate opportunity arose.

I had a little bit of "defender of the universe" in me. I felt—and still feel—that there's a higher intelligence up there, something greater than us, something we might have to answer to, and most people would be wise to keep that in mind as they hurry through their day.

And if there's not a higher power, no one's going to be worse for the wear for his or her effort.

Was there one way?

No, not as far as I could tell—other than to feel loved, to love back, and to do the things that make you feel as if your life has meaning and value, which can be as simple as making sure you spend time helping make life a little better for other people.

I decided if I could manage that I wouldn't have any serious problems were there to actually be a Judgment Day.

I found a kindred spirit in the church's youth minister, Charlie Brown. Bright, energetic, and forward thinking, he was active in Young Life, a group that ran summer camps for junior-high and high-school kids. The idea was to get kids on the right path. It was spiritually influenced but not religious; they didn't cram religion down anyone's throat. It was about walking the walk, and Charlie did that with a grace and conviction that impressed me.

It interested me, too. He was young himself. He surfed with the kids, he hung out with them, and he talked their talk.

At that time, being able to relate to young people was especially important. A younger generation was questioning traditions,

biases, and social covenants. New ideas were surfacing and clash-
ing with the old. It was clear that the world, as most of us born
before World War II knew it, was in flux. That point had been
driven home on November 22, 1963, the day President John F.
Kennedy was assassinated. I had returned to the set from lunch
in the commissary with a few people from the show and immediately noticed a change in the atmosphere.

I will never forget it. The usual lightness in the air had disappeared, and the mood was somber and heavy. We all knew immediately that something had happened, something bad and dire. I
looked around, trying to figure it out, and then someone asked if
we had heard.

"No," I said.

"The president was shot."

"JFK?"

"Yes."

We were all stunned.

I turned to Carl, John, Morey, Rosie—everyone. JFK assassinated? Dead? It was unfathomable. All of us shared an expression
that conveyed the same sense of disbelief, horror, and tragedy
unfolding in front of our eyes. We couldn't do anything but stare
at the television and mutter, "Oh my God."

Later that night, I went to the recording studio and made my
first album, *Songs I Like*. Although it was the last thing I wanted
to do that evening, and I'm sure the musicians shared that senti-
ment, we went through with the recording session anyway, and
the resulting album, at least to me, sounded that way.

In the months that followed, I found myself, like the country
as a whole, in a serious frame of mind and searching for answers
and meaning. Many nights I stayed up until two or three in the
morning, talking with Charlie Brown about why Kennedy had

been killed, why such an act of violence happened in our country, where it stemmed from, what it meant, and what we should do about it.

As was often the case, I heard myself asking questions that I had asked many times in the past: Who were we as a country? Who were we as human beings? What was really important in life? What do we tell our kids and future generations to make sure they do better?

As a middle-of-the-road Democrat, I knew where I stood. I was pro civil rights. I was against the Vietnam War. In fact, with two boys nearing draft age, I was deeply worried about the escalation of the fighting there. I didn't see the point of the United States being there. Margie was also active in a group called Another Mother for Peace.

When President Kennedy's former press secretary Pierre Salinger ran for the U.S. Senate from California, I joined his campaign efforts. He had been flying to Japan when JFK was slain and then worked briefly with Lyndon Johnson. After leaving the White House though, he returned to his native California and defeated Alan Cranston in the primaries. He ran against former actor George Murphy, a Republican.

The cornerstone of Salinger's platform, which I very much agreed with, was his opposition to Proposition 14, a ballot effort intended to overturn the California Fair Housing Act, legislation that had been passed the previous year. It prevented property owners from discriminating for reasons of race, religion, sex, physical limitations, or marital status.

My sense of the way people should be treated was thoroughly offended by those who supported overturning the proposition. I loathed bias of any kind. How could people support such measures? How could Americans openly support the right to discriminate for reasons of race, religion, and so on? Salinger was asking the same questions and fighting the good fight. I didn't know him until I pledged my support, and I grew to like him very much.

At one point, Dan Blocker from *Bonanza,* several actresses, and I were on a whistle stop tour from L.A. to San Diego, and at a speech in Orange County, we were met by a pro–Prop 14 crowd that pelted us with tomatoes and eggs and held up signs displaying vile slogans of hate.

In San Diego we attended a dinner with some of Pierre's wealthiest backers. I happened to be sitting next to Pierre when one of the bigwigs told him that he had to drop his opposition to Prop 14 and stop talking about fair housing if he wanted a shot at winning. If he didn't, the backer said, he and several others were going to drop their support.

Pierre didn't flinch.

"I can't do that," he said. "I'm running on that platform. It's fair, it's right, and I believe in it."

Hearing that, I admired him even more as a politician and as a man. Not enough voters shared my opinion, though, and he lost the election and went on to a successful career in journalism.

At work, Carl was excellent at pushing the boundaries in subtle ways, like acknowledging that Rob and Laura were intimate, as husbands and wives are, or allowing others to venture into new and dicey territory. For instance, the third season had opened with the Persky and Denoff–written episode "That's My Boy?" In it, Rob recounts how he had believed that, after Ritchie was born, he and Laura had brought the wrong baby home from the hospital. He insisted on meeting the other family, and in the end they turned out to be black.

It was a brilliant, socially relevant twist to an extremely funny episode. Initially, though, the network rejected the episode, explaining that a family sitcom was not the place to address the issue of race. However, Sheldon persuaded the network's executives to change their mind, and we all were proud of that episode's message.

Work was a great place to search for, and occasionally find, answers to some of life's big questions. Failing that, it was just a great place to be. As I told a group of people one day in a question-and-answer session for *Redbook* magazine, "Material success isn't too important [to me]. I suppose it would be if you were a businessman or a broker making investments and the money you accumulated was the symbol of your success."

But that wasn't me. I was fairly simple and basic. "I like acting," I said. "I like my work. I just love it and try to get better if I can."

15

SEEING STARS

Paris was supposed to be partly a vacation—and it was, sort of. I went there to make the movie *The Art of Love*, a comedy about a down-and-out artist who fakes his death to increase the value of his work. With Angie Dickinson, Elke Sommer, and James Garner costarring, and Norman Jewison directing, it looked like a good time. I arranged for Margie to join me on location, since we had never gone on a proper vacation other than our honeymoon to Mount Hood. I envisioned us visiting the city's museums, restaurants, and sites.

However, as with all of life, whether you're making a movie or running to the market, there are the plans you make and there is the way life actually unfolds. In this case, shortly after we checked in to the palatial Raphael Hotel off the Champs-Elysées, I had to shoot a scene where my character fled from the authorities after getting word that he was to be guillotined. We did numerous takes. For days, I ran behind a camera truck. For someone who smoked heavily and enjoyed cocktails and wine at night, I was not in terrible shape. But this was different. I may as well have been training for a marathon.

Upon returning to the hotel after work, I encountered Margie waiting to go out with me. We had museums to see, cafés to visit, and stores to peruse. But I would look down at the ground to avert her expectant gaze and shake my head pathetically. I couldn't walk. I could barely stand. So she trudged off alone while I slipped into a hot bath and soaked my achy muscles.

After that scene was behind us, our time improved. Carl also came over to act in a small part, rewrote major portions of the script, and added erudite amusement to the day. The only serious blemish on our otherwise well-deserved vacation occurred when a tabloid printed a story that I was having an affair with Angie Dickinson. They followed that with a story that Jim Garner and I had gotten into a fight over her.

Both stories were complete fabrications, containing not one single morsel of truth beyond the fact that we all were making a movie together. This was the first time I had been snared in the ugly trap of celebrity gossip and it offended me in countless ways.

After the movie, I tried to sue the publisher. I went to New York and gave a deposition, though a judge threw out my suit, explaining that libel laws were applied differently to public figures. The decision didn't make sense to me. Just because I was a celebrity didn't mean a patently false and damaging story hurt my family or me any less. It was clearly unjust.

Although I bristled over that for a long time, it turned into one of those moments that forced me to gather my wits, adjust my perspective, and basically mature. It was a life lesson—a wake-up to the fact that, as I wrote at the beginning of this book, you can't spread peanut butter over jelly. The whole thing made me relish the good fortune I had of returning to *The Dick Van Dyke Show*. It was like pulling into a safe harbor after weathering a storm. I was home.

What went unspoken was that this was the show's fourth season and from the outset Carl had said we were going to do only five. I didn't even want to think about the end. None of us did.

As an ensemble, from crew to actors to Carl and the writers, we were just hitting our stride. Episodes like "My Mother Can Beat Up My Father," which showed Laura trying to best Rob in the art of self-defense, gently but pointedly tapped in to the currents of social change. So did "A Show of Hands," in which Laura and Rob accidentally dye their hands black before attending a formal dinner. Other episodes that addressed everyday family issues, like Ritchie dealing with a girl who had a crush on him, continued to showcase Carl's genius for mining laughs from suburban living rooms and kitchens.

My brother returned for another two-parter, and I was deeply amused when Jerry Belson and Garry Marshall wrote "Young Man with a Shoehorn," an episode in which Rob becomes part owner of a shoe store and struggles as a salesman, based on a story I told one day about my own failure selling shoes in my uncle's store. I was paid three dollars a day plus commission if I sold a hundred dollars' worth, which I never did. The work was maddening. I would put twenty pairs of shoes on a woman, all of which fit perfectly, and she would walk out shaking her head that none of them was right. God, I hated that job.

One of the most memorable episodes we did that season and also one of the funniest was called "Never Bathe on Saturday." In it, Rob and Laura go away for a romantic weekend—a second honeymoon, as those types of getaways were called. After being shown into their luxurious suite, Rob grabs his wife by the waist with a hungry look in his eye.

"Darling," she says, "what about the bellboy?"

"You first," he says.

The risqué line got big laughs—and so did the rest of the show, depicting their weekend taking an abrupt downhill turn after Laura's big toe gets caught in the bathtub faucet. Behind the scenes was a little less funny. Mary had decided to quit smoking earlier in the week and she hadn't had a cigarette for several days. She was white as a sheet, shaking and nervous—like anyone going through nicotine withdrawal.

As an actress who was pretending to be stuck in the bathtub behind a locked door, she did not get much camera time. Normally it wouldn't have bothered her, but she was on edge, a rarity for Mary. At one point she even had kind of a tiff. I was so startled that I said, "Mary, will you please go outside and smoke a cigarette."

She scrunched up her face, looking frustrated but adorable and funny, and all of us laughed.

Aside from the opportunity to work, the most enjoyable upside to the celebrity I received from starring on a top-rated TV series was entrée to some of my idols—the greats who had inspired me. I took full advantage of this and developed a good friendship with Stan Laurel, though my first introduction to him happened purely by chance.

We were shooting the second season of the TV series, and I was at home one day, looking up a name in the telephone book, when I came across the name Stan Laurel.

"Stan Laurel?" I said to myself. "It couldn't be."

But I called the number. A man answered promptly.

"Hello," I said. "This is Dick Van Dyke. Is this Mr. Laurel?"

"Yes, it is," he said.

It turned out that Stan knew the show and knew who I was. He invited me to the Santa Monica apartment he shared with his fifth wife, Ida Kataeva Raphael, a Russian woman who kept a careful eye on him. As I walked down the hallway and approached his door, it suddenly opened and there he was.

"Hello, Dickie," he said.

I could not have been happier as I shook the hand of my idol. He'd had a slight stroke, but I never saw any noticeable effects as he led me inside.

My visit was everything I could have hoped for. I tried to take it all in without being rude. His Academy Award was displayed on top of his TV set. He had a small typewriter on a modest desk that was covered with fan mail, which he answered personally, though he acknowledged being months behind. I asked if he still wrote sketches or ideas, and he answered, with his famous nod, "Yes, Dickie, I do, when they come to me."

As a lifelong fan, I couldn't resist asking him questions, and he generously let me ask whatever I wanted. I asked him about my favorite movie of his, *Way Out West*. As he recalled some of his scenes with Oliver Hardy—whom he still referred to as Babe— playing prospectors trying to find gold, he sounded as if they had made the film a few years earlier, not in 1937.

Stan also confirmed that he did not like scenes in which he had to cry, even though they turned into his signature. To get Ollie to do his slow burn, Stan took advantage of his partner's love of golf. Knowing that Oliver always wanted to finish the day in time to play at least nine holes, he saved for last the scenes where Ollie lost his temper and did his slow burn. As soon as he noticed his partner getting anxious about missing his tee time, he shot them.

"I hated to cry, though," Stan told me. "I didn't think it was funny, either."

Of course, Stan thought Oliver was the funniest guy in the world. That, he said, was the secret to their partnership. Ollie made him laugh. I nodded. He didn't need to say any more. I understood perfectly.

It was, I explained, why I had become a fan, and in some part why I had wanted to get into show business. Stan made me laugh, and I had wanted to have the same effect on other people.

Before I left, I invited Stan to come see us shoot *The Dick Van Dyke Show*. We were getting ready to shoot "The Sam Pomerantz Scandals," an episode that featured the cast putting on a variety show to benefit a friend, and it included a sketch with me and actor Henry Calvin as Laurel and Hardy. I explained that everyone on the show would be honored if he were able to attend. But he politely declined, saying he wasn't up to it.

I didn't push. I knew that he never went out in public.

After the "Pomerantz" episode aired in early March 1963, I called Stan up and asked for his opinion. Knowing that he was going to watch, I had gone to great lengths to be as meticulous as humanly possible to get every detail right, and I thought I did a pretty good job, too. Stan agreed. But then he spent the next forty minutes reviewing my performance and giving me notes. He said that he had always used paper clips as cuff links. He also said that he always took the heels off his shoes, which was what gave him his trademark stance and walk. He went on and on, talking about the smallest of small details. It was the best lesson in comedy I had ever heard. I wish I had taken notes.

"You did a good job," he said. "It was the best impersonation I have seen."

"Thank you," I said.

"There is one more thing," he said.

"Yes?"

"The hat was a little off," he said.

"I knew it," I said. "Yours and Ollie's had flat brims. Mine curled slightly. I tried to find one like yours. I even tried ironing the brim on my derby."

He laughed.

"Young man, why didn't you just ask me?" he said. "You could have used mine."

"Oh my God," I said.

"Well, God bless," he said, and then he hung up.

O n February 23, 1965, Stan died after suffering a heart attack. Reporters came to my house for comments. As I stood in the front yard giving interviews, a sprinkler burst, causing me to jump and dance around while getting soaked. I was sure it was Stan's doing, one last funny bit. He left his derby to me, though it was never found among his belongings.

Still, I was immensely touched. To me, it was like the passing of the baton, both an honor and a responsibility.

His funeral at Forest Lawn brought out Hollywood comedy legends Buster Keaton, Hal Roach Jr., Patsy Kelly, and Alan Mowbray, among others, but at the request of Stan's wife, I delivered the eulogy, which I began by stating what to me was the obvious: "Laurel and Hardy are together again—and the halls of heaven must be ringing with divine laughter."

Stan did not want his funeral to be a solemn occasion and in fact had written a warning to all of us: "If anyone at my funeral has a long face, I'll never speak to you again." Buster Keaton reportedly told people that Stan was the funniest of all the great film comics, funnier than Chaplin, funnier than even himself. I could not have agreed more.

"In the wee hours of one of his last mornings on Earth," I said in my eulogy, "a nurse came into Stan's room to give him emergency aid. Stan looked up and said, 'You know what? I'd lot rather be skiing.' The nurse said, 'Do you ski, Mr. Laurel?' He said, 'No! But I'd lot rather be skiing than doing this.'

"Stan once remarked that Chaplin and Lloyd made all the big pictures and he and Babe made all the little cheap ones. 'But they tell me our little cheap ones have been seen by more people through the years than all the big ones. They must have seen how much love we put into them.'

"And that's what put Stan Laurel head and shoulders above all the rest of them—as an artist, and as a man. He put into his work that one special ingredient. He was a master comedian and he was a master artist—but he put in that one ingredient that can only come from the human being, and that was love. Love for his work, love for life, love for his audience—and how he loved that public. They were never squares or jerks to Stan Laurel.

"Some of his contemporaries didn't criticize Stan favorably back in the thirties. Some of his contemporaries took great delight in showing their tools, and their skills, their methods on the screen; they were applauded because the audience could see their art.

"Stan was never really applauded for his art because he took too much care to hide it, to conceal the hours of hard creative work that went into his movies. He didn't want you to see that—he just wanted you to laugh, and you did!

"You could never get him to pontificate about comedy. He was asked thousands of times, all through his life, to analyze comedy. 'What's funny?' he was always asked, and he always said: 'How do I know? Can you analyze it? Can anybody? All I know is just how to make people laugh.'

"That's all he knew!"

I ended with the recitation of a poem of unknown authorship that I had come across years earlier, "The Clown's Prayer."

> *God bless all clowns.*
> *Who star in the world with laughter,*
> *Who ring the rafters with flying jest,*
> *Who make the world spin merry on its way.*
>
> *God bless all the clowns.*
> *So poor the world would be,*
> *Lacking their piquant touch, hilarity.*
> *The belly laughs, the ringing lovely.*
>
> *God bless all the clowns.*
> *Give them a long, good life,*
> *Make bright their way—they're a race apart.*
> *Alchemists most, who turn their hearts' pain,*
> *Into a dazzling jest to lift the heart.*
> *God bless all clowns.*

I met Buster Keaton the same way I did Stan. I found out that someone I knew had his phone number and one afternoon I called him up. His wife, Eleanor, answered and put Buster on. After a short talk, he invited me to lunch. He lived in Woodland Hills, about ten minutes from my Encino house. He had a beautiful piece of property, maybe a quarter of an acre.

While Stan was very much an English gentleman, he was still gregarious and friendly. Buster was the opposite. He was extremely shy. After meeting him, in fact, I was surprised I had been invited out. His wife greeted me at the door and chatted with me in the kitchen. After a while, I saw Buster through the kitchen window. He was walking around outside. His wife smiled the patient smile of a woman who knew him well.

"He'll come to you," she said. "Give him time."

Sure enough, he finally entered the kitchen. He had on his flat hat and was playing a ukulele, singing, "Oh Mr. Moon, Carolina moon, won't you shine on me." He was more comfortable in character, as the showman, or talking about his work. I asked if he remembered the bit where he put one foot on the table and then the other and we saw him suspended in midair before he fell. Not only did he remember, at age sixty-eight, he did it for me, then and there.

Way out in the back he had a little picnic table where we had lunch. A miniature railroad ran through the yard. Buster made hot dogs for us and ran them out to the table on the train. He got a kick out of that. On another one of my visits, we were in the kitchen when his dog, a giant St. Bernard named Elmer, sauntered through the back door, looked up at Buster, then at me, and let out a loud and clear meow.

"How the heck did you get him to do that?" I asked.

Buster opened the dog's mouth and pulled out a newborn kitten. It was soaking wet from the dog's slobber.

"It's in his mouth like a wad of chewing tobacco," I said.

Buster laughed.

"He found the kitty and has been taking care of it," he said. "He carries it around like that."

I also learned Buster was something of a pool shark. He had

a specially built table and custom-made pool cues. We played a couple games and he massacred me. Given that the cues had his name on them, who would have expected any other result? In fact, he ended up leaving those cues to me after his death in 1966.

I gave the eulogy at his funeral as well. All the same people from Stan's funeral the previous year were present again, everyone except Buster.

My connection to the older stars extended to Harold Lloyd, who wanted me to play him in a movie, and a number of actors from Hollywood's Golden Age whom I met on visits to the Motion Picture Home, where characters like Babe London treated me to stories about Charlie Chaplin, W. C. Fields, and Harry Langdon. I also met one of the Keystone Kops, a man in his eighties whose hobby was making costume jewelry. One of his customers turned out to be a wealthy widow. He ended up marrying her and living out his life in luxury.

Talk about happy endings.

16

UPSETS AND GOOD-BYES

I n the spring of 1965, I made *Lt. Robin Crusoe, U.S.N.,* a silly Disney movie about a Navy pilot who ends up on a deserted island with a native girl and a space program–trained chimp for companionship. The picture was pure family fun—and a good time for me personally for a reason I never expected: I fell into a deep friendship with the chimp.

We shot a good portion of the movie in Kauai and made a family vacation out of it. Walt and his wife, Lillian, came over, too. We stayed at a hotel whose accommodations looked like grass-covered huts. Walt and Lilly had the room above ours, and I heard him hacking and coughing all night. Yet after dinner, as we told stories in the bar, he smoked like a chimney, and drank pretty well, too, as did I in those days.

My partner and manager, Byron Paul, was directing the movie, and before shooting on the first day, my costar Nancy

Kwan, a beautiful actress originally trained as a classical ballerina, took him aside and asked, "Mr. Van Dyke is not going to bother me, is he?" Evidently she had been in another project where someone had spent the entire production chasing after her.

"No, Mr. Van Dyke is safe," Byron told her.

She needn't have worried, as Mr. Van Dyke was occupied with his other costar. A jungle set was built near the beach, and on the first morning of work, as I walked onto the set holding a Styrofoam cup of coffee in one hand and a cigarette in the other, I was greeted by Dinky, the 130-pound chimp who was the real star of the movie. Seated in his personal director's chair, which was near mine, he crooked his index finger and motioned me toward him.

"Hello, how are you?" I said.

Apparently he felt the same way I did. After a slight roll of his eyes, he reached for my coffee and cigarette, then drank the coffee and smoked the cigarette. I looked at his trainer.

"He shouldn't smoke," I said.

"Neither should you," the trainer said.

From then on, I brought Dinky a cup of coffee every morning and lit a cigarette for him. I might as well have asked him how he slept, as we started our days so similarly. It was as if we could actually talk to each other. Soon Dinky and I started to have lunch together. He ate with a fork and used a napkin. For a chimp, his manners were impeccable. So was his sense of humor.

One day I saw him resting cross-legged on a log. I noticed he had taken off the chain that was normally around his ankle and put it around the leg of his trainer, Stewart. I swear he caught my eye and gave me a look that said, *Don't tell.* All of a sudden he took off and ran up a tree, then beat his chest and laughed.

I don't know any other way to describe it, but Dinky was chuckling at his own joke.

I was charmed. He started to have a thing for me, too. He would pick at my hair the way chimps do with one another. I would get down on the ground to make it easier for him. When he finished, I went through his.

He developed an obsession with my watch. I almost expected him to know how to tell time—that's how bright this chimp was.

In the movie, he played golf and he was incredible. We also played poker. One day he was sick. I think he had a temperature of 103. In the scene, we were playing cards. He was supposed to be able to see my cards in the shaving mirror behind me. Amazingly, he looked up and smiled on cue. But the second that Byron said *Cut,* he would groan and lay down, ill.

I turned to the trainer and Byron. I wanted the trainer to help him and Byron to praise him. This chimp was a pro.

The downside was that when he misbehaved, his trainer took him away and hit him. I hated that. In one scene, I came sliding down a coconut tree as planned, but I startled Dinky, who was seated at the base of the tree. I saw all of his hair suddenly stand on end. So did Stewart. He balled up a chain he kept with him and threw it at the chimp. He saw the look on my face. It was one of surprise and anger.

"He would've attacked you," he explained.

I never got used to that part of working with the chimp. To me, he was a doll. I forgot that he was an animal being cajoled, if not forced, into performing acts that did not come naturally to him. Later I heard he was doing a Tarzan movie in Mexico and bit an actor in the face. I was told the actor picked him up and pinched him, and in turn Dinky nipped his face. That was the end of his film career.

He was ten years old, so he was pretty close to retirement, anyway. After I heard he'd been placed in the Los Angeles Zoo, I went there to see him, knowing he had been raised in a house his whole life—he had never been in a cage. When I got there, he was sitting in the middle of a large circular pen. It was outdoors, but it was still a cage—and I saw the effect it had on him.

I called out his name. He looked up and recognized me immediately. He ran over as close as he could. I could tell from the expression on his face that he was asking me to get him out of there. It looked like he was saying, *I'm in here with a bunch of monkeys. Take me home.*

The whole visit upset me. I knew he thought that I had come to take him out, which I would have if it had been possible.

I had to walk away. I couldn't look back.

There was a similar feeling of sadness when it came time to acknowledge the end of *The Dick Van Dyke Show*.

In late summer of 1965, all of us began the fifth season knowing it was our last. The public may not have realized it yet, but we knew.

Carl felt strongly that he would get stale after five years of writing and rewriting thirty-nine episodes a season, and so would the show. He thought all of us would lose the spring in our step. I think he also recognized that all of us, through our collaboration and hard work, had produced a TV classic, and he feared that if repetition and fatigue set in, it could tarnish the show's magical reputation. He also may have been ready to do something else.

The same may have been true of Mary. She may have been ready to move beyond Laura Petrie. I don't know. But I doubt it.

Was the show getting stale?

No.

Repetitive?

No.

Was I ready to leave?

No.

I loved the show and the people. It wasn't work. I played myself. Between the series and a movie every summer, I had a great setup. As a performer, nothing topped the excitement and energy of working in front of a live audience. If it wasn't the stage, a weekly show like ours was as close of an approximation as one could get. We stopped only if there was a mistake or a scene change. Otherwise the studio audience let us know if we were funny or not.

If there was discussion about continuing the show without Carl, I didn't hear it. Ownership issues aside, I couldn't imagine anyone considering *The Dick Van Dyke Show* without Carl Reiner. Although it was a collaborative effort, everything about the show stemmed from his endlessly and enviably fascinating, funny, and fertile brain and trickled down to the rest of us. We all knew it, and as each of us said in our own ways, we appreciated every aspect of having been party to this chapter of television genius.

The final season began airing in September. Two months later, CBS put out a press release informing the rest of the world what we already knew—that this would be the show's swan song, its final season. I got steamed when the *New York Times* attributed the decision to me. It wasn't true. Not wanting the disappointment of millions of viewers pinned on me, I did a series of interviews with other reporters wherein I tried to explain I wasn't behind the decision while still holding the party line, namely that we wanted "to quit while we were still on top."

It was like yelling into the wind, though. The writers still stared back with perplexed looks, as I'm sure our fans did, too, asking yet again, "So why are you all stopping a hit show?"

I was not as hard-pressed to answer the other question people asked—what next? In February 1966, I was being interviewed by a reporter who asked that question—"What are you going to do next?"—with such concern that I had to tell her not to worry, I was going to be fine.

Indeed, I had a full plate of TV specials and movies. I had invested in a Phoenix-based radio station. I also volunteered with Big Brothers, served on the board of the National Conference of Christians and Jews, worked with the California Educational Center, donated time to the Society for the Prevention of Blindness, and of course cared for my wife, four children, various dogs, and our ornery cat. But really, until *The Dick Van Dyke Show* finished, I preferred to concentrate on, no, I preferred to savor, each and every last episode.

L ike the others before it, the final season continued to take in-spiration from our personal lives. Carl's earliest literary efforts were the source of "A Farewell to Writing," which has Rob struggling to begin the novel he always wanted to write. In "Fifty-Two, Forty-Five or Work," Rob recalls a time when he was out of work with a new home and a pregnant wife, and that story-line was ripped straight out of my family album.

Likewise, "The Man from My Uncle," about government agents using the Petries' home to stake out a neighbor, may have sounded far-fetched, but the script from Jerry Belson and Garry Marshall was rooted in another actual event that happened to me. After the Watts Riots in August 1965, I gave some of my time to Operation Bootstrap, a group that endeavored to help people in Watts develop skills and businesses of their own without government aid.

They began on a shoestring budget in a former auto-parts store and eventually gave rise to the Shindana Toy Factory, a business that designed toys for African-Americans. I made several trips with members from my church to the empty store where Bootstrap was headquartered, engaged in some heated debates, and got to know this one guy named Lenny.

In his thirties, Lenny was a member of the Black Panthers, extremely political, but also extremely thoughtful and sensitive. I learned that he was a painter. He showed me his canvases, which I admired. I also found out that he was married and had a daughter. On those levels at least we related to each other easily, more than one might think given our different worlds.

Interested in bridging those different worlds, I invited Lenny and his family to my house for dinner with my family. My kids were fascinated by Lenny. He was fairly articulate but tough as nails, which was reflected in the stories he told during dinner. Those stories pinned the kids to the table. I mean, nobody moved while Lenny spoke—that is, until the phone rang.

I answered and a detective from the LAPD identified himself and told me not to worry, they had things under control.

"What do you mean?" I asked.

"We heard there was going to be an armed robbery in your house tonight," he said.

"What?!" I exclaimed.

"We have your house surrounded," he said.

"Holy Jesus!" I said, looking across the room at Lenny and cringing at what he was going to think.

After I hung up, I told everyone what was going on. Lenny erupted in anger, got up, and walked toward the phone.

"I'm going to make a call," he said. "In two minutes I'll have forty guys here with guns."

"What?" I said.

"We'll take care of them," he added.

"Dick!" said Margie, who had gotten up from the table and was now standing next to me. "Do something."

First, I calmed the situation inside my house, and then I walked outside and dealt with the police. There were cops everywhere. I had no idea where the LAPD got their information, whether a neighbor saw Lenny and his family enter our house and called the local precinct or whether it was a mistake, which seemed unlikely. But I was pissed—and embarrassed.

While the memorable evening did eventually morph into a good TV episode, I wish it had turned out differently.

As for the series finale, an episode titled "The Gunslinger," it was a Western spoof in which Rob goes to the dentist and gets put under, descends into a dream, and everyone is transported back into the Wild West. We cooked that up so that everyone could be in the last one: I was the sheriff, Mary was the song-and-dance girl in the saloon, Carl was the bad guy (Big Bad Brady), and all the writers (Sam, Bill, Jerry, and Garry) were cowboys. Even my children were in it.

We added to the fun with a cast and crew party afterward. As hard as we tried to celebrate five special years of accomplishment, camaraderie, creativity, friendship, and laughs, it was also a night of good-byes, which made it a bittersweet occasion. I got in the car at the end of the night, turned to Margie thinking I had something to say about the party, and nothing came out of my mouth. I was overwhelmed.

I learned that you may move on from a show like ours, but you never move away from it. At the end of May 1966, we staged a mini reunion when the show walked away with four Emmys. The *New York Times* called it "a hail and farewell gesture" by our peers since we were going off the air. Indeed, almost everyone on the show had been nominated. We were genuinely touched.

I arrived at the awards show thinking Don Adams was a shoe-in for his new series *Get Smart,* and so I was genuinely caught off-guard when my name was called for the third straight year. In my thank-you speech, I joked that I wouldn't be there next year, so the category was going to have a fresh face. I added a heartfelt thank-you, which I hoped conveyed my gratitude not just for the individual honor but also for the honor of being there.

And it was quite a club. That night, Bill Cosby, one of Emmy's cohosts, also won an Emmy for his work opposite Robert Culp on *I Spy.* The first black actor to costar in a weekly prime-time TV series, he thanked NBC for "having the guts" to go with him. It wasn't just NBC, though. It was also Sheldon Leonard, *I Spy's* executive producer, who had put Bill in that role and who had, at another point in time, fought to keep *The Dick Van Dyke Show* on the air.

When you're watching award shows you sometimes wonder what the men and women in their tuxedos and gowns are thinking about while all the nominees are being called and winners announced. On that occasion, I was thinking about the connections many of us shared as we strove to entertain and inform

people, and occasionally make points about the quality and condition of our lives, and I felt pretty darn lucky to be among them.

I was also thinking that I was on to the next phase of my life
and career, some of which was planned, but most of which was a
mystery, the way it always is, and I was looking forward to seeing
what would happen.

PART TWO

I've made peace with

insecurity...

because there is no security

of any kind.

—Me

✦

17

NEVER A DULL
MOMENT

D estiny is an interesting idea to ponder. Somehow, when Carl was looking to cast the lead role in his new television series, I was in the exact right place at the exact right time and answered the call. However, such was not the case one day in 1966, a day that, had I answered in another way, could've made me far wealthier than I ever imagined.

I was in the driver's seat of a Volkswagen Bug parked in front of a McDonald's, biding my time on the set of the movie *Divorce American Style* while the crew completed a routine recalibration of equipment and director Bud Yorkin conferred with my costar Debbie Reynolds. A man sidled up to my little car, introduced himself, and asked if I lived in Phoenix.

"I don't exactly live there," I said. "But I own a ranch outside of town. We're there a lot on weekends."

He then explained that he was with McDonald's and they were selling franchises in and around Phoenix for twenty-five thousand dollars for each restaurant. McDonald's wasn't exactly unknown. At the time, there were about five hundred places fronted by golden arches across the country, boasting sales of one hundred million hamburgers. But I thought twenty-five grand for a burger joint was steep. So I passed.

Fortunately, I had better judgment with Hollywood than hamburgers. Case in point: *Divorce American Style*. It was a sprawling, topical comedy written by Norman Lear, with his partner, Bud Yorkin, helming the production. Debbie and I played a husband and wife whose marriage was on the rocks after they'd carved out a successful life for themselves in the suburbs. In other words, they had achieved the American Dream, but at a cost—their relationship.

The script, which also included parts filled by Jason Robards, Jean Simmons, Van Johnson, and Shelley Berman, was a hefty three hundred pages, more than double the standard length. The studio had told Norman the film couldn't possibly be that long. His response was along the lines of: "It's my story, and by God I'm going to make it the way I see it."

Norman's wife, Frances, was a smart, opinionated woman who, I'm going to guess, gave him good source material on the ever-shifting state of marriage. But then everyone seemed to be going through *something*. Debbie was in the middle of her second marriage, and she was, in addition to being a strong woman herself, and a teller of colorful stories about Hollywood, also a handful who regularly informed me that I didn't know anything about making movies.

In a way, she may have been right. One day I did something

terribly stupid. I was shooting a scene with actor Joe Flynn, best known as the captain on *McHale's Navy,* and I was supposed to get drunk following a frustrating situation with my wife. After a handful of takes, I said, "What the hell, get me a real martini," and three hours, numerous takes, and a couple of martinis later, I was smashed.

So much so that Norman drove me home. All the way there he asked, "Why did you do that? Are you crazy?"

I wasn't the only casualty on the movie. One day we shot a scene with Pat Collins, who was known as "The Hip Hypnotist." She was supposed to hypnotize Debbie, who then climbed onstage and performed a sexy dance. It was pretend, of course, except that cinematographer Conrad Hall, who later won an Oscar for *Butch Cassidy and the Sundance Kid,* and several of the grips actually fell under Pat's spell. Filming stopped while she brought them out of their trances.

At lunch that day, Van Johnson asked Pat to help him quit smoking. They did one session and he never smoked again. I ran into him years later, though, and he was about fifty pounds heavier. He was still off cigarettes, he explained with a smile. But he had a new vice—Häagen-Dazs ice cream.

From *Divorce American Style,* I went directly into the movie *Fitzwilly,* a light comedy costarring *Get Smart*'s Barbara Feldon. Despite Oscar-winner Delbert Mann's direction, the movie flopped and, as film buffs can attest, will likely be remembered only as composer John Williams's first collaboration with Marilyn and Alan Bergman.

Next, I tried to make a movie out of the book *Fear on Trial,*

John Henry Faulk's nightmarish account of being blacklisted. For whatever reason, I was unable to get it off the ground. Even with Norman Lear and Bud Yorkin attached as producers, the subject matter may have been too controversial for the networks. In 1975, it was finally adapted as a TV movie with George C. Scott and William Devane in the starring roles.

Then it was back to television for me, with my first special for CBS, which aired in April 1967. The network billed it as a homecoming, though it bore little resemblance to *The Dick Van Dyke Show*. Nor did it resemble a traditional variety show. I wanted to do something different and daring, instead of a theme and a bunch of guest stars, and the most different and daring idea I came up with was to challenge myself to do it all—or most of it, anyway.

Some may have thought it indulgent.

To me, it was fun.

Loads of it. I opened the hour-long show with a zany, silent-film era–style montage of my trying to get to the studio after my car breaks down. I kayak, roller-skate, skateboard, and ride in a golf cart, finally arriving onstage clinging to my car bumper.

I had only two guests. One was my old Merry Mutes partner, Phil Erickson, who leapt at the chance to take a week off from running his comedy club in Atlanta and reprise our old act on network television. In one bit, we pantomimed to the Bing Crosby–Mary Martin hit "Wait Till the Sun Shines, Nellie" (including the earthquake that punctuated our act nearly twenty years earlier), and in another titled "A Piece of Lint, or How Wars Begin," we played two friends who get into a skirmish after one of them picks a piece of lint off the other.

Whether the audience enjoyed it (and I think they did), we had a blast. Backstage we joked that it was nice knowing our timing was still intact after a fifteen-plus-year break, in case we needed a fallback.

My other guest star was Ann Morgan Guilbert, who'd played Millie on *The Dick Van Dyke Show*. In one of my all-time favorite skits, I played "The Great Ludwig," the world's oldest magician, and Ann was my dedicated assistant and wife. The skit was supposed to go eight minutes, but funny business kept happening—as she levitated, for instance, I ad-libbed, "Why are there flies around you?" which made her crack up, and then I lost it. The tails of my tux were set on fire, which was planned, though I pretended not to notice, which inspired more shtick—and, well, it ran for nearly fifteen minutes.

Ann and I left the stage with tears in our eyes from laughing so hard, the tails of my tux still smoking! We thought it was hysterical, brilliant, serendipitous comedy magic. Then the director came up to us and said, "We're going to have to redo it."

My jaw dropped.

"What?" I said. "What's the problem?"

"We saw the boom [microphone] in the shot for a few seconds," he said.

"We can't re-create that stuff," I said. "It just happened. We'll have to use it as is, mistakes and all."

Stuff kept on happening, too. I played a flamenco dancer who crashes through a piano, a musician reinterpreting Bach as jazz on the harpsichord, and reworking *Fiddler on the Roof*'s signature number as "If I Were a Rich Man." All in all, it was "a splendid showcase," said the *New York Times*, and the *Pittsburgh Gazette* patted me on the back by writing "It should have been longer."

If only reaction to *Divorce American Style* had been as complimentary. It wasn't the critics who blasted the movie, though. It was my fans. They felt I had betrayed them by taking on a role in which my character got drunk in one scene and dallied with a prostitute in another. The headline in the *Los Angeles Times* captured the shock: NEW VAN DYKE FILM CHANGES HIS IMAGE.

I refused to see that as a problem since I wasn't doing anything that crossed the line of decency I had set for myself.

"Let's face it," I told Roger Ebert. "Debbie Reynolds isn't Tammy anymore, and neither am I."

B ut the question nagging at me wasn't "Who am I" as much as it was "Who did I want to be?"

Like a lot of people when they reach their forties, I was trying to figure out the answer. Although my oldest child was headed to college and I still had three others at home, I was mulling a change of some sort. I didn't know exactly what, but I envisioned myself retiring and, if not getting out of show business, then slowing down. In fact, in an interview with *Redbook* magazine, I mentioned that I might retire in six years and work with youth groups.

Why?

I was restless and felt the need for something more. As I explained, I was "looking for meaning and for value, personal value."

How could I feel that way when I had a wonderful wife, terrific children, a thriving career, a shelf full of awards, and strangers approaching me every day just to say they were fans?

I suppose those are the nuanced inklings that precede midlife crises and keep psychiatrists in business. In order to deal with them before they turn into full-blown problems, though, you have to be attuned not just to the initial feelings, but also to the need to address them, and I wasn't.

For me it was business as usual. I went to work on the movie

Never a Dull Moment, a comedy about an actor who gets into trouble after he's mistaken for a gangster. My pal Jerry Paris directed, and we laughed every day on the set. The picture also allowed me to work with the great character actor Slim Pickens, who showed me how to throw a punch, and screen icon Edward G. Robinson, who grinned at every person who wanted to shake his hand.

It turned out he was stone deaf.

One day I asked if he'd ever tried a hearing aid. Grinning, he pulled out a tiny sack and let me look inside. It contained five hearing aids.

"None of them work," he said.

"Why don't you get them fixed?" I asked.

"Sorry," he said. "Can't hear you."

From there I went straight into *Chitty Chitty Bang Bang,* a movie that I repeatedly turned down. Based on Ian Fleming's only children's novel, it's the story of an eccentric inventor whose magical automobile is coveted by foreigners with nefarious intentions. The movie's producer, Albert "Cubby" Broccoli, known for his tight-fisted control of the James Bond movie franchise, desperately wanted to re-team Julie Andrews and me.

I can't speak for Julie's reasons, but both of us turned him down. I thought the script had too many holes and unanswered questions. However, each time I said no, Cubby came back with more money. I'm talking serious money—more than seven figures, which in those days was mind-boggling, plus a percentage of the back end, which I never counted on.

I still wanted to say no, but my manager reminded me that not too many years earlier I was scrambling to win two hundred dollars on *Pantomime Quiz*. Although I was in a different position now, I understood—and just in case I didn't, he let me know if I turned down this much money I was basically declaring myself officially crazy.

After one more round, I finally agreed.

In the interim, Cubby hired the remarkable Sherman brothers to write the score, as well as my favorite choreographers, Marc Breaux and Dee Dee Wood. While both additions pleased me greatly, I made one last stipulation. I didn't want to reprise my English accent, which I'd struggled famously with in *Mary Poppins*. Not a problem. My character was suddenly an eccentric American inventor.

In lieu of Julie, the role of Truly Scrumptious went to another Yank, Sally Ann Howes, who truly was. From a show business family, she arrived with a long list of stellar credits, starting at age twelve when she worked with Vivien Leigh in the film *Anna Karenina*.

Cubby Broccoli wanted an extravaganza, as was his way, and he spent more than double what it cost to make *Mary Poppins* to ensure he got one. Spanning ten months, production was headquartered at London's Pinewood Studios, but also touched down in Bavaria and the South of France. For some reason, my hair curled as soon as I arrived in London and few of the English crew even recognized me. In fact, as the film's opening racetrack scene was shot, the assistant director walked through a crowd of extras, handing out flags they were supposed to wave as the cars passed, and he gave one to me, too.

"But I'm in the movie," I said.

"Not yet, mate," he replied. "But you will be if you wave that pennant when the camera is pointed at you."

I limped through my actual opening scene, having injured my-self while shooting the dance routine for the song "Toot Sweets," an over-the-top production that took three weeks and involved an army of dancers, singers, musicians, and one hundred dogs. It was my stupidity. While trying to keep up with all the twenty-year-old dancers, I did not warm up properly and paid the price.

It turned out I had a torn calf muscle, but the doctor gave me a more serious diagnosis, arthritis. According to him, my arthritis was so pervasive that he predicted I would be in a wheelchair within five to seven years.

I did not let that bleak prognosis get in my way, but I did have to put any dancing on hold until my leg healed. The most demand-ing number we shot also turned out to be one of my favorites, the song "Me Ol' Bamboo." Marc and Dee Dee ended this exuberant dance by making us leap over our sticks and roll directly into a somersault. It looked great. But it took twenty-three takes for everyone to execute the moves correctly and at the same time.

As I did the final one, I felt my cuff catch on my heel. I thought, Uh-oh, and pushed through with all my might. I did not care if I ripped my pants and pulled them halfway down my legs. I could not have done a twenty-fourth take.

We began working in and outside of London, and we spent quite a while there, enough time that Margie and I attended a royal screening of the new James Bond film, *You Only Live Twice*. I stood in a receiving line with Sean Connery and others, waiting nervously to meet the Queen of England, all the while reminding myself of the etiquette briefing we'd received, the most important rule of which was to not speak until the queen spoke to us.

Not that it mattered. At the moment she stepped toward me, her eyes making contact with mine and a smile forming on her lips, Jerry Lewis, standing behind ropes to the side of me, called out, "Hey, Dick!" I turned and said, "What?" as the queen stood in front of me, waiting to be acknowledged. I was mortified and have never gotten even with Jerry for causing that ill-timed distraction. Nevertheless, the queen greeted me warmly and said, "We very much enjoy your television show."

Soon after that June gala we relocated to the South of France due to a lack of sunshine in England. We'd sat around all day for weeks at a time, waiting for the sun to break through the clouds so we could shoot a scene, but the clouds refused to give way. Finally they said this was going to have to do. If you pay careful attention to the movie, you will see us driving through what is supposed to be the English countryside, except there are vineyards all over the place.

The car itself, aka Chitty Chitty Bang Bang, was hard to drive. It had a four-cylinder engine that coughed and sputtered in real life, and the turning radius of a battleship, but we still had a lot of fun in it.

Off-camera, I enjoyed myself even more. In France, where we took over a resort in St. Tropez, Margie and the kids and I went on long hikes through the countryside. When we switched locations to Rothenberg, Germany, I took guitar lessons and spent every Sunday afternoon in the town square listening to musicians play Bach, which sounded beautiful in the outdoors. They played with a fervor that still puts me back in that square every time I hear one of the Brandenburg concertos.

Midway through production, I became acquainted with John A. T. Robinson, best known as the Bishop of Woolwich. I had written him a fan letter, explaining that I was an American actor who admired his book *Honest to God*, and I would love to meet him if he had time while I was in Europe. He contacted me right away and we had such a good time talking that we decided to cohost a thirty-minute radio program once a week.

The show might have been better if we'd been of differing opinions, but I agreed with his thesis that God was not an all-powerful "cosmic superman" looking down from the penthouse as much as He was Love. The bishop put it more eloquently in his book when he wrote, "Assertions about God are in the last analysis assertions about Love."

As far as I was concerned, that cut to the very heart of faith, belief, and the way to live. If knowing, finding, and giving love were the paths to knowing God, I thought people could get there without much additional doctrine. Maybe an occasional push back in line or a gentle slap on the wrist. Otherwise it was pretty clear and simple.

That did not, by any means, conclude that life itself would be simple—and it wasn't. As we shuttled between London and the South of France, Margie suffered through a series of health problems that finally got the best of her when a local doctor surmised she might have cervical cancer. I didn't need to hear anything else. After months of being there with me, she took the kids back home and underwent a series of medical tests.

When I told Cubby that I needed to go home and be with my wife while she had more exams, he understood and wished me well. He said that he'd do the same if he were in my position. Before I left, he even put his arm around me and said, "Don't worry. We'll shoot around you."

I was gone only a few days. Margie's tests came back negative and I jetted back to Europe only to have my agent inform me that Cubby had docked me eighty thousand dollars for missing work. Furious, I didn't want to talk to him after that, which wasn't good since I was already unimpressed with the director, Ken Hughes.

Quite simply, I thought he was wrong for the picture. One day I heard him grouse that he had to rewrite Roald Dahl's script. Who rewrote Roald Dahl?

Soon after I heard him swear in front of the children one too many times, and I finally had words with him. Above all else, it showed that he had no feel for the family-oriented material. As for the material in general, let's just say that enough scenes were done on the fly or redone at the last minute that I lost faith that the version that finally showed up in theaters would match anyone's expectations, and I think I was right.

As far as I was concerned, in the end, *Chitty Chitty Bang Bang* suffered from everything I feared at the outset, lack of story and substance. I know the film is beloved by many, but for me it lacked the magic of *Mary Poppins,* which its producer had hoped to emulate. What saved *Chitty,* at least in my opinion, were the brilliant Sherman brothers, whose title song earned them another Oscar nomination, and Marc and Dee Dee's choreography, though I have to note the *New York Times* was much kinder in its review, echoing the feelings of many in calling it a "fast, dense, friendly children's musical."

If that's the case, as I thought at the time, I'll gladly take it.

18

SOME KIND OF NUT

I returned home from Europe to a different—and difficult—time. It was early 1968, an election year and a period of unrest, confusion, conflict, upheaval, and ultimately great sadness. I never thought being in show business made me immune from the things that affected everyone else, and I wasn't, starting with the news that Charlie Brown, the charismatic youth minister at my church, had taken a new position in the Pacific Northwest.

His departure changed the dynamic inside the church and caused me to slowly drift away from there and from organized religion in general. The clincher occurred during a meeting of church elders. We were puzzling over what to do about the racial problems that kept much of the city divided. One of the elders suggested inviting the congregation from a black church from the inner city to our church and, ideally, they would invite us to theirs. I thought it was a great idea, right on target. It sounded like something that would have come from Charlie, who preached the best possible way, by example. The things he did the other six days of the week were far more inspirational than anything he said on the seventh day in church, which was also pretty good.

"Black families, white families, people in general—we look at each other like strangers," I said. "But I think we have much more in common than any of us realize. We sit in our churches on Sundays, we read from the same book, we pray to the same God, we want the same thing, which is to feel loved, not hated. What if we got to know each other through an exchange program?"

The idea did not go over well. One of the elders emphatically stated that he did not want any black people in the church. Appalled, I stood up, shared my disgust, grabbed my jacket, and walked out. I never went back there or to any other church. My relationship with God was solid, but the hypocrisy among the so-called faithful finished me for good.

My faith was tested again in April when Dr. Martin Luther King Jr. was assassinated. Like many Americans, I took the tragedy personally. I knew and admired the man and his mission. A few years earlier, I'd had the honor of meeting Dr. King at a rally in Los Angeles, where I was also among the speakers.

It was a large event at the L.A. Memorial Coliseum. Rod Serling, the genius behind *The Twilight Zone* and an early civil rights advocate, got me involved and also wrote my speech, which articulated my feelings about being a God-loving human being in the latter half of the twentieth century and moving beyond backward and bigoted thinking.

Moments before we filed through the locker room tunnel and went onto the stage in the middle of the field, a security official informed us that there'd been a threat on Dr. King's life. He said that we had the option of backing out, and everyone would understand if we did. No one fell out of line.

We marched out and gave the most impassioned speeches of our lives, at least I did, though I have to admit that when Dr. King sat next to me, I did lean slightly to the other side.

At the time Dr. King was assassinated, I was involved in the organization Concerned Democrats and was campaigning on behalf of Senator Eugene McCarthy's 1968 bid to become president of the United States. Being on the campaign trail with McCarthy brought back memories of when I was a teen and my grandfather took me to the train station to see Wendell Wilkie speak in his run against Franklin Roosevelt in 1940. My grandfather was against the New Deal and referred to Roosevelt as a "One Worlder."

It's likely he would have been against McCarthy, too. But I was attracted to his stance against the Vietnam War. He was the first candidate to publicly question the war and call it a mistake while defending his patriotism. He was also a poet and unusually sensitive and personable for a politician. At a fund-raiser in Minneapolis, I became separated from him and his group as we snaked through a crowd. Suddenly, he stopped, turned, and asked, "Where's Dick?"

I caught up and asked how he knew that I'd fallen behind.

"I had a sense," he said.

That pretty much describes what I really liked about him. He had a sense of what was going on in the country and what ought to be done to ensure a brighter tomorrow for future generations. He won the New Hampshire primary, which caused President Johnson to take himself out of contention. Sensing an opening, though, Robert Kennedy entered the race. With rolled-up shirtsleeves and youthful vigor, he ran against McCarthy.

In June 1968, I was with the McCarthy camp at the Hilton hotel in downtown Los Angeles, waiting for the results of the California primary. Bobby Kennedy was about a mile away at the Ambassador Hotel. I was briefly distracted from the night's main event when actress Myrna Loy showed up in the same dress that my wife had on. Myrna was quite charming about it and both women ended up having a good-natured chuckle.

Then I found myself in a corner talking to someone about my fears that McCarthy was too smart and too intellectual and not a tough enough politician to get elected. I said he reminded me of Adlai Stevenson, who had lost in two elections to Eisenhower. Sure enough, Bobby Kennedy topped McCarthy in the state's Democratic presidential primary. The mood in our ballroom, which had been poised for celebration, was downcast and disappointed as we followed Kennedy's victory speech from down the road on TV.

Moments later, we were frozen in time as news reached us that Kennedy had been shot. I remember shock, despair, and tears.

"Not again," I said to Margie as we held each other and waited for news on Kennedy's condition.

He died the next day—and with him and Martin Luther King Jr., the country lost much more than two great leaders, and although many of us knew that, we did not know how to fill that void.

In August, I followed McCarthy to Chicago for the Democratic convention. The sight of Mayor Daley's police lining the street and appearing to taunt demonstrators made me feel as if we had already lost the war three months before the battle for the presidency. Afterward, I retreated to our Arizona ranch, where Margie and I spent weekends and summers with the children.

We had 180 acres in the middle of the desert, and it was the perfect place to decompress. We had been lured there a few years earlier to the area outside of Phoenix by our friends Marc and Dee Dee, who had a place nearby. Margie fell in love with the desert. I had expected to find a small A-frame on a couple of acres. Instead, we ended up with a ranch whose property sprawled farther than I could see. It was a special place with unique charms. I could do nothing for hours and found endless fascination staring up at the billions of stars that filled the clear nighttime sky.

For me, work was the best antidote to the problems I saw plaguing the world. I was so lucky that I loved what I did and was able to make a good living at it. In addition, it provided me with a sense of giving back something of value. If you could entertain people and take them away from their problems for a while, you were doing pretty well, I thought.

With two movies and a TV special in the works, I was doing just fine. The first film was *Some Kind of a Nut,* a comedy written and directed by Garson Kanin, whose erudite sense of humor had defined his screenplays for *Born Yesterday, Pat and Mike,* and *Adam's Rib.* In *Some Kind of a Nut,* he cast me as a banker who grows a beard after getting stung by a bee and developing a rash, but he sees his career and personal life suffer drastic consequences when, in a stab at independence, he opts to keep his facial hair.

I enjoyed working again with Angie Dickinson, who was a doll, as were Rosemary Forsyth and Zohra Lampert, but the partnership with Garson, who was lovely and came to the set each day dressed to the nines, didn't work out as I had hoped. It was nothing he did or didn't do; the material, envisioned as a social satire, just never panned out. It "sounds like something out of Kanin's trunk," said the *New York Times*. I knew it, too. Even as we shot a scene with Rosemary where we rolled around in Central Park, I said to myself, "This is terrible . . . it stinks . . . but it's Garson Kanin . . . how can this be?"

Ah, well. I had higher hopes for my next picture, *The Comic*, an homage to old-time silent-movie comics and idols of mine like Stan Laurel and Buster Keaton. A labor of comedy love from my old cohorts Carl Reiner and Aaron Ruben, and directed by Carl, this picture costarred Mickey Rooney and Michele Lee and told the story of silent-film star Billy Bright (loosely based on Keaton, but really a composite of several of those guys) as he looked back from the grave on his life and career.

Like any clown, he had as many private torments as laughs— maybe even more—but making the movie was like a playdate with friends who appreciated this special era of comedy and all its subtleties as much as I did. In his book *My Anecdotal Life,* Carl wrote, "I believe, if Mephistopheles popped in on Dick and offered him a chance to sell his soul for the chance to work in those old black-and-white comedies, he would think long and hard before refusing."

He was right. But this was my chance to go back in time, and I took full advantage of it. Carl and Aaron Ruben and I were like kids let loose in a video arcade. It was playtime. We rewrote every day. Why wouldn't you with those two in the room? Also, we couldn't help ourselves. During production, we got together every day, looked at the script, told one another stories, laughed, and pretty soon someone said, "Why don't we do this instead?"

For me, the best part was re-creating Billy Bright's shtick. We shot it on sixteen-millimeter black and white, speeded it up so it would look authentically old, and then dragged the footage across my backyard to mess it up. Of course, we shot much more footage than we ever needed just because it was fun. Carl and I also talked about doing something with the extra material. We didn't know what that might be, but something.

Unfortunately, all of that footage disappeared sometime before the movie opened and never resurfaced. I've been heartbroken since. Yet the picture itself buoyed my faith in the effort we put into it. Upon its opening in November 1969, the *New York Times* called the film "genuinely funny," the local *Los Angeles Times*' critic Kevin Thomas said it was "one of the most devastating films ever made about Hollywood," which he meant in a good way.

I n April 1969, after I had completed both films but months before either of them were released, I starred in my third special for CBS, which was my most delightful special quite simply because it costarred Mary Tyler Moore, the most delightful costar of my career. When *The Dick Van Dyke Show* ended, we vowed to get together for lunch every three weeks. It never happened. Busy schedules, career demands, and family obligations made such a well-intentioned promise impossible to fulfill.

But the feelings were always there. Countless times I spoke about the good fortune I had in continuing to work with Carl, Aaron, and others from the show. However, I missed the daily interaction and laughs I got from Morey and Rosie, and I especially missed my partnership with Mary, which made working together again such a treat for me.

Like me, she had done a handful of films, but thanks to the considerable success of our show and its continuation in reruns,

Mary was still primarily thought of as my on-screen wife, a perception that short-changed her considerable talents. Our special, titled *Dick Van Dyke and the Other Woman,* set out to change that. Produced and written by Bill Persky and Sam Denoff, along with Arnold Kane, the show was an hour of dance and comedy that was meant to play easily and show off Mary.

I told Bill and Sam to let her do whatever she wanted, and I tossed in a few suggestions of my own, too. Hey, I would have been nuts not to take advantage of singing and dancing with Mary.

"It's my chance to fool around with her," I joked.

In one scene, Mary and I played a couple on a wedding cake, and in another she did a tour-de-force dance through the history of the modern woman, from the flapper era to the start of women's lib. We also took a moment to acknowledge the show that made us household names, when I strolled into the *Alan Brady Show* office—all of the set had been in storage at CBS. I played it with a wink and a smile, as if I were taking the viewers at home back to a familiar time and place, which of course I was.

"I wish I had a nickel for every hour I spent here," I said, and then, after a brief pause, added, "Oh, I guess I do."

Mary got her own series the following year. *The Mary Tyler Moore Show* debuted on CBS in 1970 and became another TV classic. All of us who knew and loved Mary expected as much from her. While she was the perfect actress for those changing times, I was, like so many people back then, just trying to keep up with them. One night my wife and I drove to Eagle Rock, just outside of downtown Los Angeles, to have dinner with our oldest son, who was studying at Occidental College. Our second oldest, Barry, was about to graduate from high school, and the girls, Stacy and Carrie Beth, were sixteen and ten.

Chris, a junior, was living off-campus in a house with his girlfriend. He had the place decorated like a hippie den, with batik-like fabrics on the ceiling and Moroccan rugs on the floor. The lights were low and there were candles lit. It was all very nice as we sat down and visited. Then my wife caught my attention and raised her eyebrow ever so slightly, a movement that was the equivalent of a dog whistle, imperceptible unless you have been trained to respond to it, but after twenty-plus years of marriage I knew exactly what it meant.

I had already taken note. In the middle of Chris's coffee table was something that looked at first glance like a vase—except it did not hold flowers. When Chris and his girlfriend went in the kitchen to prepare dinner, I turned to Margie and whispered, "It's a bong."

"A bong?" she asked.

"For smoking marijuana," I said, quickly pantomiming someone taking a hit off a joint before Chris returned and saw me.

Margie's eyes were full of concern and questions. Was Chris smoking pot? How did her straight-arrow husband know about this? I assured her that I'd never tried pot, and I was just as curious as she was. Over dinner, though, the four of us talked about everything except the one subject we wanted to talk about most. I don't know how Margie and I managed to ignore the two-foot-high water pipe on the coffee table behind us, but we did.

Then we got in the car and it was like the dam burst.

"Oh my God, he's smoking pot," Margie exclaimed. "What's going on?"

"I think he's smoking pot," I said.

19

TIIE NEW DICK VAN DYKE

S peaking of smoking, I smoked too much. While I also consumed too much alcohol, I had yet to recognize it as a problem. But cigarettes were different.

In 1964, the U.S. Surgeon General came out with a report that linked smoking cigarettes to cancer, and it was as if that report spoke directly to me. I had smoked a pack or two every day since my late teens. I knew that I needed to quit smoking cigarettes. But knowing you have a problem and actually doing something about it are two different things, and it took me six years from the time the Surgeon General released his report to finally making a concerted effort to quit.

I tried on my own, and then I tried every device and program that came on the market. It may as well have been a full-time occupation. First, I went to SmokEnder, and when that failed I signed up for an even more intense program called Schick. There, they put me in a phone booth—sized room, sat me in a chair situated by a big tub of sand full of cigarette butts (yes, as if I was in a giant ashtray), and instructed me to smoke.

"You want me to smoke?" I asked.

"Yes," the counselor said. "A whole pack."

"A pack of cigarettes?" I said.

"Yes." She nodded. "And do it as fast as possible."

The idea was to have the smoker overdose on nicotine, get seriously ill, and create an association in the brain that cigarettes were bad. It was severe, extreme, and sudden behavior modification.

I became ill just thinking about it, but I did it. A dutiful scout, I smoked an entire pack as quickly as I could and immediately got violently, grossly sick to my stomach. I was dizzy, nauseous, and an ugly shade of green as I staggered outside the room and into the hall, where I was met by my counselor and another of the Schick attendants, both of whom were clearly inured to the sight of people holding on to the wall so they did not keel over.

"Man, what an ordeal that was," I said.

Then, without thinking, I reached into my pocket and took out a cigarette.

The attendant turned ghostly white.

"Here's your money back, Mr. Van Dyke," he said.

I was not the only person I knew who was trying but failing to quit. I heard all sorts of stories. It struck me that millions of people across the country were also struggling with the same filthy habit, and I thought the story of someone going to great lengths to give it up might make a good movie. I wrote up an idea and gave it to Norman Lear.

As I knew from working with him on *Divorce American Style*, Norman had his finger on the pulse of the culture—and the sense of humor to find what's funny in the pathetic helplessness of all those who knew they were killing themselves every time they lit up. I also knew that he was a smoker who had tried umpteen times to break the habit.

After reading my treatment, Norman called me up and said he couldn't write a story about one guy. He didn't see it carrying an entire movie. But it had given him another idea, one that he thought would work better. Instead of one guy trying to quit, what if it was an entire town?

Norman explained that he had read Margaret and Neil Rau's novel *I'm Giving Them Up for Good,* a cynical satire about a disingenuous cigarette company's brilliant PR ploy of offering $25 million to a town that can quit smoking for an entire month, knowing full well that no town can possibly quit, since cigarettes are addictive. That, along with my idea and Norman's own futile efforts, made the subject ripe for satire.

"That's brilliant," I said.

Before long we had decamped to Iowa to make the movie *Cold Turkey,* one of Norman's best and I think most overlooked comedies. It falls into that category of biting social comedies that range from *Catch-22* to *Thank You for Smoking.* In the movie, I played the Rev. Clayton Brooks, who leads the town of Eagle Rock, Iowa, in their effort to meet the tobacco company's challenge. A first-rate team of comics and funny actors rounded out the cast, including Bob Newhart as the cigarette company's opportunistic PR man, Tom Poston as the town drunk, Jean Stapleton as the mayor's nervous wife, and Bob Elliott and Ray Goulding—better known as Bob and Ray—as TV newsmen from New York who descend on the town to cover the drama.

It was just as funny off-screen. Norman started the picture smoking a pipe, as did I. Both of us were using the picture as a motivation to quit. He was, in fact, having a better time of it than I was. He had about two weeks—that is, until it came time to shoot a scene featuring a room full of people, all locals cast as extras, who were chain-smoking fiendishly. There was one woman who wasn't a smoker and it was obvious. So Norman showed her how to do it.

"No, you take it like this," he said, putting the lit cigarette in his mouth, "and then you inhale like this."

Well, as soon as he took that first drag, I saw his eyes glaze over. Before the day was finished, he had smoked an entire pack.

I wasn't much better. One day I decided to drive to Danville, but I underestimated the distance and forgot to check the gas in a car I borrowed, and I ran out of fuel in the middle of nowhere. A neighborly farmer came to my rescue. On the way to the gas station, he offered me a cigarette. I said no thanks and explained that I had quit.

"I've quit fifteen times myself," he said while lighting up. "It's impossible."

"You're right," I said.

I was soon smoking again, too. But I tried to keep it to a minimum. As a way of distracting myself, I rented a Harley-Davidson motorcycle and rode it to the set every day. I found the fifteen-mile drive to be an invigorating way to wake up. On one of my rare days off, I rode into the northern part of the state. While exploring the countryside, I came upon a ceremonial gathering of members from the Sac and Fox Nation in a remote part of the woods.

Although this didn't appear to be an event for non–Native Americans, I stopped and watched from the edge—that is, until the chief spotted me. He turned out to be a fan of *The Dick Van Dyke Show*. He invited me in, and I ended up eating dinner and dancing with them late into the night. Before I left, they made me an honorary member of the tribe, dubbing me White Bear. Later, many of them attended the premiere of *Cold Turkey* in Des Moines.

A few months later, Margie and I were exploring the perimeters of our Arizona ranch when we spotted a pile of what seemed like oddly shaped stones. They turned out to be pieces of Native American pottery, stone jewelry, and arrowheads. Some researchers from the University of Flagstaff recognized the relics as belonging to the Hohokam, a tribe that disappeared from the area in the 1400s. Hohokam, we were told, was Pima for "the vanished ones." But our discoveries showed they were not entirely gone.

I loved thinking about these people who had inhabited our land hundreds of years earlier. Just the fact that it *had* been inhabited. If you looked in any direction, the land appeared barren, empty, yet it obviously wasn't. There were shadows from another time. I had always been fascinated with the bigger picture, and here was a connection to it.

We decided to move to the ranch full-time. After the Encino home sold, Stacy and Carrie Beth started new schools in Scottsdale. For Margie and me, it was probably the beginning of the end of our marriage, though we had no inkling of it then. Cognizant of Margie's dislike of Hollywood, I convinced myself that I could live anywhere and still work, and looking back, I did enjoy the quiet and solitude on the ranch more than I had imagined.

People never believed me when I described myself as lazy, but I could spend hours sitting on the rocks under the large desert sky, following birds as they rode the thermals up and down like an

My brother Jerry and
me in the backyard.
My father had piled up
a bunch of rocks and
called it a garden.

My mother, maternal
great-grandmother,
and me at about age
two or three. I don't
remember the man in
the picture.

My cousin Phyllis
and me at my
Aunt Katherine's
wedding. We were
the flower girls.

My fourth birthday,
sitting atop a pony.

Out on Hazel Street in 1933, in my backyard—surrounded by my cousins Phyllis, Helen, Betty, and Neal, and brother Jerry.

My dad, Jerry, and me shortly before I went into the service. My dad had finally switched to a four-in-one tie.

With Chita Rivera in the
Broadway production of *Bye
Bye Birdie*, 1960.

Being silly on the set
of *The Dick Van Dyke
Show*, 1962.

Left: Mary Tyler Moore and me in costume for "The Doodlin' Song," performed on *The Dick Van Dyke Show*, 1963.

Below: Mary, me, Sheldon Leonard, and Carl Reiner with our Emmy awards for *The Dick Van Dyke Show* at the 16th annual Television Academy awards, 1964.

The cast and crew of *The Dick Van Dyke Show* begging the sponsor to pick us up again. Carl Reiner is at the top, with my assistant Frank Adamo and Jerry Paris beneath him. Morey Amsterdam is on my left.

Above: With Julie Andrews in rehearsal for *Mary Poppins,* 1964.

Left: Julie, helped by turtles, keeping me afloat in "Jolly Holiday."

Left: Me (Bert the Chimney Sweep), Julie (Mary Poppins), Karen Dotrice (Jane Banks), and Matthew Garber (Michael Banks) in "Chim Chim Cher ee."

Below: With the chimney sweeps in "Step in Time." We rehearsed for weeks in the sweltering San Fernando Valley summer heat. Darned near killed me, but it was worth it.

Above: At Grauman's Chinese Theatre, putting my hands and footprints in the cement, June 1966. *Below:* The family band.

Right: Gathered around a harpsichord my wife had just bought me for my birthday.

Below: With Walt Disney. One time we were interviewed and the reporter asked about us being on opposite sides of the political fence. Walt said, "That has nothing to do with our friendship." I always appreciated that.

Meeting Queen Elizabeth as Sean Connery looks on. The Queen said,
"We enjoy your show very much."

Sally Ann Howes and I take the kids for an unconventional ride in *Chitty Chitty Bang Bang*, 1968.

Above: With President Johnson, getting a proclamation for the Brotherhood of Christians and Jews. *Below:* At the L.A. Memorial Coliseum, listening to Dr. Martin Luther King, Jr.

Above: An out-of-control moment with Carl Reiner, who was a guest on *Van Dyke & Company,* 1976. I was wearing my hair longer. Carl was wearing hair.

Left: With another Emmy, this time for *Van Dyke & Company,* 1977.

With Mary Tyler Moore after I was honored for lifetime achievement at the American Comedy Awards, 1993.

Dick Martin, Dom DeLuise, me, Steve Lawrence, and Richard Crenna in my living room. Steve was the only good voice in the bunch.

Above: My daughter Stacy and me on an episode of *Diagnosis Murder,* 1996. Michelle hated that moustache more than anything, but I thought it made me look like a doctor.

Left: With Chita Rivera, 2006. I made several guest appearances in her Broadway show, *Chita Rivera: The Dancer's Life,* more than forty-five years after we appeared together in *Bye Bye Birdie.*

invisible roller coaster, and thinking about life. The broken pottery littering the ground confirmed for me that material success, although great, was not the be-all and end-all. There was more.

I didn't know the answers, but I could feel that the things that gave life meaning came from a place within and from the nurturing of values like tolerance, charity, and community.

I nurtured more than values, though, when I added ten head of cattle to the ranch. I bought them just to tell people that I had cows. Cows from neighboring ranchers already grazed on our land; I wanted my own. As they ate in the late afternoon, I sat next to them on hay bales and sang country songs while accompanying myself on the guitar. I knew four chords—enough to play almost any country song. The cows were like a nightclub audience. They stared and chewed.

Our menagerie also included four quarter horses, a Great Dane, and a pinto horse named Frijoles who thought he was a dog. He visited our back door throughout the day, hoping to get invited inside. He let the kids play on him as if he were a puppy, and ran next to me like a circus horse when I rode my dirt bike. He spent all his time looking for opportunities to play with us.

One summer night we had a family cookout way down in the pasture. As we prepared dinner over the fire, Frijoles sniffed at our steaks as they cooked in the skillet and burned the hell out of his nose. Poor guy. He wanted to be part of the family so badly.

While riding my dirt bike one day, I made a discovery that let me go back to work without going back to Hollywood. I was speeding down a dirt road that led off the ranch and into town where I picked up the mail, but sticking to the path I detoured across a dry arroyo and came upon the nearly completed Carefree Southwestern Studios, a complex of four soundstages for movies and TV. Workmen were putting the finishing touches on it.

"Why hadn't I heard about this place?" I asked myself. I only lived about eight miles from the site.

But now that I knew about it, I saw things differently. I called both my agent and manager, Sol and Byron, and said that I could accept the longstanding offer from CBS to do a series. They were shocked and asked the reason for my sudden change of mind. I told them about the studio.

"Are you nuts?" Sol asked. "Why do you want to do a series in the desert?"

"So I can ride my minibike to work," I said.

"That's crazy."

Crazy like a fox.

In the spring of 1970, I shot an NBC special with Bill Cosby there and things went so smoothly that CBS agreed to let me do a new weekly sitcom from there, too. Carl signed on as executive producer and came up with the premise for the show we called *The New Dick Van Dyke Show*. I played Dick Preston, a local TV talk-show host living in Phoenix with his wife and family. That it sounded similar to the original series wasn't an accident.

But Carl made it clear that he was not interested in writing another series. That job went to Saul Turtletaub and Bernie Orenstein, two top comedy scribes who'd just ended five years on Marlo Thomas's hit series *That Girl*. The hardest part of the whole process of putting the show together was pitching the idea to actors—not the idea of the show, but the idea of moving to the desert.

We lucked out when Hope Lange accepted the part as my wife, Jenny. I liked Hope on her previous series, *The Ghost and Mrs. Muir*, on which she'd worked with my old friend Charles Nelson Reilly and also, not insignificantly, won two Emmys. She was also a real dame, with a career that included the movies *Bus Stop* and *Peyton Place*. She'd also had a long-term relationship with Glenn Ford.

As my agent said, there was a lot to like about Hope, and I agreed, especially when she joined us in the desert.

The supporting cast was rounded out by teenager Angela Powell as our daughter (another child was written to be away at college), Fannie Flagg as my sister, David Doyle as the station boss, and Nancy Dussault and Marty Brill as our neighbors. We set up shop on Stage 1 and rehearsed until a rhythm and chemistry emerged—not something that was guaranteed when you put a bunch of strangers together. But this group had talent on- and off-camera. Nancy was a well-known singer, Fannie was starting to write fiction (she would publish the bestselling novel *Fried Green Tomatoes at the Whistle Stop Café* in 1987), and Marty was an amateur astronomer and former concert pianist, which captured my interest as a devoted self-taught noodler who could fritter away half a day playing jazzy chord progressions.

One day I noticed that Marty was missing a finger, and I wondered how he could still manage to play complicated pieces. He had lost the finger in an accident, he explained, then retaught himself to play.

"The fickle finger of fate," he quipped, referencing a popular line from *Rowan & Martin's Laugh-In*.

That reminded me of my own fateful story, which I proceeded to tell him.

One night after a taping of *The Dick Van Dyke Show*, I was driving home on Sunset Boulevard, and as I rounded the bend near UCLA known as "Suicide Curve," I lost control of my car, a new Jaguar XKE. The back end spun out and all of a sudden the car itself was spinning and there was a crash. I had no idea exactly what else happened.

When everything stopped, the car's body and all four wheels were gone—basically scattered, blown out, or disintegrated—and I found myself sitting on the chassis. I undid my seat belt and got up. The guy who had been driving behind me rushed over to me. He said I careened off the road, hit a wall, spun in the air, and landed right side up on the street. The only things that held together were the engine and me.

Even though no one else was involved in the wreck and there was nothing to report, the police showed up. They asked me who was driving the car. I said that I was.

"No," one of the cops said. "Whoever was driving the car is dead."

You would have thought. But I was unbelievably, and inexplicably, lucky. My hair was perfectly combed and my suit and tie looked as they had earlier when I left the studio—at least from the front. When I turned around, the cops pointed out that the entire back side of my suit was ripped to shreds. It turned out I had a slight concussion, and the next day I was too sore to move, but in all the ways that mattered I was perfectly fine.

"How does that relate to the show we're doing?" Marty asked.

I laughed.

"It means you never know what's going to happen," I said. "You do your best, then take your chances. Everything else is beyond our control."

"Yeah, but how do you think we're going to do?" he said.

20

THE MORNING
AFTER

M argie and I were vacationing in London when *The New Dick Van Dyke Show* debuted on September 18, 1971. I heard the reaction was positive. A few days after we returned, though, I was in the grocery store when a sweet-looking woman walked up to me and hit me with her purse.

"Excuse me!" I said, stepping back before she could do it again.

"How dare you leave that sweet Laura," she said.

It wasn't exactly the kind of hit I hoped for, but it told me that people watched. In fact, despite lukewarm reviews, including the *New York Times,* which said, "on the originality meter, it rated two, maybe two-and-a-half, coughs," we were a Top 20 show. Of course, it helped to be in a Saturday-night lineup that included America's number-one show, *All in the Family,* as well as *The Mary Tyler Moore Show* and Sandy Duncan's new series, *Funny Face.*

Carl wrote and directed the opening episode, but from then on it was always a struggle behind the scenes to fill the scripts with the requisite funny. Although it was never mentioned, all of us knew that in addition to battling for ratings, we were competing against the extraordinarily high expectations my previous show set. People like the woman in the grocery store saw more than just a new sitcom. We tried our best to deliver.

Hope was not used to working in front of an audience, and so on taping nights when the studio was packed with people who had driven in from Phoenix to see the show, she calmed her nerves with a little belt. That one drink made her happy enough to do the show.

Sometimes it made her even happier. We were doing a scene in an episode midway through that first season where I came home from work and found her already in bed. I changed clothes and walked around to get into my side of the bed. When I pulled back the covers, she was stark naked. The audience hooted and laughed, as did Hope, who thought she could make me crack. But I never went out of character even though I thought her prank was hilarious.

During the second season, Hope was involved with Frank Sinatra. One week he came out to visit her. He flew in on his Lear jet and set up camp in the little house that she rented. Hope invited a bunch of us over for dinner one night and Frank cooked. We went there after taping the show. Margie had come to the studio to drive there with me, and she was all excited about meeting Frank.

It was funny, because it wasn't like she'd never met big stars before. We had attended every major awards show. I'd made movies with some pretty famous people. But as I've said before, my wife did not like Hollywood, its stars, or its emphasis on status. To put it another way, she was not a fan of the tinsel in the town. Hence, we were living in the middle of the desert.

On the way to Hope's, I said something to that effect. Margie gave me a look as if I had started to speak a strange language.

"But this is Frank Sinatra," she said.

We walked in and were immediately hit by the thick, garlicky aroma of a rich Italian meal. I knew it was going to be a good one. Hope led us into the kitchen, where we were introduced to the man responsible for the delicious smell filling the house. Frank was at the stove, with his shirtsleeves rolled up, and wearing an apron. He had made the entire meal from scratch. Friendly and loose, he fixed drinks and served us dinner.

It was an evening of food, booze, stories, and laughs— everything except the one thing Margie wanted from Frank, to hear the famous Sinatra voice. Throughout the whole night, she tried to get him to sing, and he wouldn't. Several times she heard him humming to himself in the kitchen. She then elbowed me, as if to say, *See, he's almost singing. Do something that will get him to sing.*

With Frank, it clearly did not work that way. He did what he wanted to do, and that night he wanted to cook pasta, tomato sauce, and garlic bread, and afterward watch us bite into his own chocolate cake. He did not want to sing.

I understood.

There was also something that *I* did not want to do. Few people would have guessed what it was. But I had a problem with alcohol. I knew that the time had come to deal with it.

It was August 22, 1972, and I was alone in the kitchen, staring out the window at the expanse of desert. I wish I could have admired the arid beauty more, but I could barely see past my throbbing headache. I took a few aspirin. As I set my water glass down on the counter, I noticed my hands shaking. This was nothing new. I'd had the morning shakes countless times before. And that was just the most visible symptom of a condition that I had, until now, done a first-rate job of ignoring and denying—a drinking problem.

I do not know how much I drank. Some nights it was three drinks. Some nights it was double that and maybe even more. But how much I drank, whether it was one or a dozen, didn't matter. The point was that I drank, and I had to face up to the fact that it was affecting more than just me. The rest of my family was suffering for it, too.

Just the night before, I had lost my temper with Margie for no reason, and now, as I sat in the kitchen sober and sore, I knew it was not the first time that had happened. Nor was Margie the only victim of such outbursts. I'd snapped at the kids numerous times, too. It was always at night and always after I had gotten in my cups.

I told myself that wasn't me. But in truth, it was me. Maybe it wasn't at one time, but I had become that person and I realized that if I wanted to be the man I thought I was, I needed to get help. That's exactly what I did. I got out the Yellow Pages and called St. Luke's Hospital, which advertised a treatment. A woman answered. I said that I had a drinking problem and wondered if they could help me.

"Yes," she said.

"Do I need an appointment?" I asked. "How do I do this?"

"Come in," she said.

"Now?" I asked.

"Yes," she said. "Now."

Margie and the children expressed concern and offered support as I packed a bag. Then I made the twenty-minute drive to the Phoenix hospital and began the process of trying to figure out how I ended up with a problem.

*A*lcoholic was not a term that came to mind when I thought about myself. For years, Margie and I did not drink. As I mentioned earlier, we kept a bottle of Early Times in the pantry for company, but neither of us ever unscrewed the top for ourselves. It was only after we moved to Brookville, Long Island, that I began to drink, and then it was only at parties.

I was the prototypical social drinker. I had a martini to loosen up. It got me past my shyness and helped me enjoy the night. Very quickly, though, I was enjoying the night with three or four cocktails, and then I did the same at home when I arrived back from work. I never drank on the set. But by the second season of *The Dick Van Dyke Show,* I would start looking at my watch to see how close we were to five o'clock. Pretty soon I just knew without having to check the time.

As soon as I got home, I poured myself a glass of bourbon. And then another. And sometimes still another. In a frank admission to columnist Marilyn Beck, I said, "Somewhere along the line I progressed from being just a party drinker to the point where I'd run a race with Margie each night to see if I could get drunk before she could get dinner on the table."

I did not get drunk—not in the way most of us think of

drunk. It was more that a couple of drinks before dinner put me in a more tranquil state of mind. And a couple more after dinner kept me in that place.

But I never thought of myself as an alcoholic.

And why was that?

Well, I would ask myself simple questions.

Did I drink in the morning? No, not unless it was a Bloody Mary at Sunday brunch, and who didn't have one then?

Did I drink at work? Never.

Did I go to bars? No.

Did I have a problem? No, not as far as I was concerned.

Others saw it differently. In 1967 a friend dropped by the house and said some people who had worked with me were whispering about my drinking. They hadn't actually seen me drinking, he said, but they'd noticed me complaining a few too many times about being hungover.

"Maybe you want to get some help," he said.

"I don't have a problem," I said. "I appreciate your concern and friendship and willingness to come to me, but I swear to you, I'm fine. I have a couple drinks at parties, one or two to unwind at night, but that's it. If that makes me an alcoholic, well, I guess everyone else is, too."

"But Dick, you understand why—"

I cut him off.

"I understand," I said. "But I don't have a problem."

The staff at St. Luke's did a double take when I walked through the doors and said I was there to check in for treatment. They were not expecting anyone famous. They kept looking out the windows for reporters. Eventually I was able to assure them that no one knew I was there. I explained that I had called earlier about getting help for a drinking problem, my wife had dropped me off, and now I wanted to be treated like anyone else.

And I was. I was placed in the psych ward with other alcoholics and drug addicts. We were separated from those with serious emotional problems, but we heard them in the background. The addicts and alcoholics were bad enough, though. Some were having fits and throwing up from withdrawals, others were agonizing through the DTs. I had no such side effects.

Although the hard-core addicts scared the hell out of me, I didn't let that get in the way of the work I needed to do. I attended group meetings daily in a basement room with concrete walls and a single lightbulb hanging from the ceiling. One day, I suggested that I didn't think I was an alcoholic, or a severe case, since I didn't have any physical problems going cold turkey. A thin, pasty guy about my age said, "Buddy, there aren't different types of alcoholics. You are one or you aren't. And you are. And it don't matter if you're rich and famous like you are or a desert rat like me. The only way to beat this thing is to put a plug in the jug. Period."

During treatment and therapy sessions, I dredged up emotions and fears I had buried long ago, like the fights my parents used to have when I was a child. I remembered hearing their screams rattling through the house. It was always after my father came home drunk following one of his lengthy road trips. Then, a little after I turned six years old, my mother gave him an ultimatum: either quit drinking or she was leaving.

She left and went to a friend's house in Boston. Then my dad went back on the road.

All of a sudden I found myself, along with my brother, at my paternal grandparents'. I had no idea where my mother and father were. I was told only that they were gone. Nothing specific was said to me (and Jerry was too young to know). I sat in my grandmother's lap at night and cried. Finally my mother returned, followed by my father, and everything was all right again. I was nearly grown before they told me the truth.

During treatment, I dealt with those painful memories for the first time and faced other more recent and regrettable issues, like the way I'd snapped at Margie and the kids over the past few months. I saw myself repeating some of the mistakes my father had made and vowed to stop. There was no instant cure, but self-awareness was the first step to real change.

After three weeks at St. Luke's, I was sober for the first time in nearly fifteen years. Feeling enlightened and empowered, I understood that alcoholism is a disease, one that does not care if you have strong moral fiber or no conscience at all, and that, like it or not, I was an alcoholic. I also understood that the disease does not quit until you do. You had to wave the white flag.

I thought that by going in for treatment I was better. I certainly had more knowledge, awareness, and the tools to help me.

But, as I would learn, that wasn't enough.

On my last day at the hospital, Margie came to pick me up. I was sitting on my bed while she spoke with the counselor in the hallway. I thought she was getting tips on what was next for me. However, after a few minutes, the counselor came in and said that Margie was taking over my room.

"What?" I asked. "She's driving me home."

"No," he said. "She just checked herself in."

It turned out Margie had a problem with Librium. She'd been taking the drug for anxiety and depression and gotten hooked. I had no idea. The situation, while serious, was ironic. We were quite a pair—a drunk and an addict. I offered the same support and encouragement she had given me, and I visited regularly over the next few weeks as she confronted her problems.

As we sobered up, the two of us began to wake up to the realities of our lives, which were more complicated than we were ready to admit.

PART THREE

You know what Dick's problem is? He always wanted to be smarter than he is.

—Jerry Van Dyke

✦

21

SAILING AWAY

S hortly after getting out of the hospital, I moved back to L.A., leaving Margie and the girls at the ranch. I commuted back on weekends, but putting that much distance between us was a prescription for future trouble.

Were there other options? I did not think so.

CBS had picked up *The New Dick Van Dyke Show* for a third season, but the network insisted on making major changes, starting by moving production to L.A. They also gave us a new time slot, on Monday night at nine-thirty, and a creative overhaul that had my character, Dick Preston, moving to Hollywood to work on a daytime soap opera after his talk show was canceled. Some critics wondered why the network didn't cancel the show in real life.

Others were even harsher. When Carl and I faced the press at the end of summer to talk about the revised premise and addition of new castmates Chita Rivera, Richard Dawson, Barbara

Rush, and Dick Van Patten, I found myself defending the fact that my hair had turned white ("I have no control over that," I said, "and I'm not going to dye it") and trying to diplomatically answer a reporter's rather nasty inquiry as to why Mary's show was a hit and mine wasn't.

"I got old," I said. "Mary didn't."

People laughed, as did I, although you could hear a sour note if you listened closely. Although comforted by the fact that Carl was more involved with the scripts, I had a hard time going back to an empty apartment after work. I had never lived by myself. I had gone from my mother to Margie. I was lonely, confused, and filled with questions about my life—or rather the meaning of it—that came as a result of my struggle to stay sober.

I hadn't liked the person I became when I drank, but I wasn't especially keen on the refurbished version, either. I felt a pretty big vacancy inside. And one night in April, after going eight months without a drink, I lost my willpower. I fell off the wagon, as they say. On my way home from the studio, I stopped at the liquor store, bought a bottle of Jack Daniel's, and poured myself a drink as soon as I got home. I did not even pause to take my jacket off.

I had three more drinks before I got sick to my stomach. I poured the rest of the bottle down the sink.

Mad and disappointed with myself, I called home and made a tear-filled confession to Margie. Then I did what any other alcoholic must do if he or she is determined not to succumb to this insidious disease: I acknowledged my slip as evidence that I was powerless over my addiction and started my sobriety again from day one.

✳

Midway through the second season we had an uncharacter-istically rocky moment when CBS rejected an episode Carl wrote ("Lt. Preston of the 4th Calvary") because it contained a scene in which Dick and Jenny's daughter Annie peeks in their bedroom and sees them having sex. The audience did not see anything other than Annie looking in the door, and in the next scene, after noticing Annie acting peculiarly, we wonder if in fact she saw us making love.

We have a talk with her, and in what I thought was a beauti-fully written moment, I explain sex to Annie as an intimate physi-cal expression of love. My character goes on and on, as he was wont to do, and he is still talking when Annie gets up and starts to leave the room. Since he's not finished, Dick asks if she has any questions.

"No," she says. "But you sure looked silly."

I thought that was the perfect response. The scene was smart, really sensitive, and funny—a classic example of Carl Reiner's trademark touch. Today no one would question the propriety of such a scene. But back then the network thought it was too ris-qué and the show was shelved except in Canada, where it played without complaint.

Incensed, Carl vowed to never again work with CBS (though he appeared in several specials in the early 1980s).

I delivered a shocker of my own to the network when at the end of the third season I met with CBS executives and said that, despite a bump in ratings, I did not want to do a fourth. I was fin-ished. Out of the previous three seasons, I explained, I counted only about seven episodes that I thought achieved the standard that I envisioned.

"I want my fellow actors to be able to work again," I said in a joking tone. "If we keep going, I might ruin their careers."

Once the series wrapped production, Margie and I fled to Coronado, a secluded jewel of an island just outside of San Diego, for a long, much-needed vacation. I decompressed and she soaked up the scenery. We took long walks along the Pacific, stared at the waves, went sailing, and talked endlessly as if we were getting to know each other all over again.

Indeed, we were trying to do exactly that. If either of us realized deep down that we might have started to grow apart, we did not acknowledge it. We were high-school sweethearts who had pledged togetherness for the rest of our lives. We had four children. And so much history together, so many stories.

And yet.

Deep down.

The knowledge that people change.

Margie wanted me to retire.

I wasn't ready to stop work. Even though I held the record for talking about retiring and then changing course, what was I going to do?

"Enjoy life," Margie said.

"I do," I said.

"Take up hobbies, like me," she said.

"I already have one," I said. "It's my job."

A couple of weeks on the beach, however, put us in a more like-minded, sympathetic frame of mind and we decided to move there. In AA they call that a geographic cure—instead of facing your problems, you simply change locations. As Margie looked for homes, I started work on a movie.

I did not expect to jump back into work, but the ABC movie *The Morning After* turned out to be one of the best and most powerful pieces of acting in my career, as well as one of the most personal. Based on Jack Weiner's novel, the script told the story of an oil company public-relations man's battle with alcoholism, something he first refuses to admit, believing he is merely a "social drinker," but then struggles with after seeking help.

It was unflinchingly raw and honest, and for that reason, I think, it was powerful, disturbing, and provocative.

I knew that I had to do it.

At the time, only a few people guessed I had a problem with booze. So it was ironic when producer David Wolper sent me the script. When I asked why me, I was told that besides having a deal with the network, I fit the type they wanted for the lead: an average, middle-aged, middle-class family man.

Before production began, I told director Richard Heffron about my battle with alcoholism. His eyes nearly bugged out of his head. But I could not have asked for better treatment or direction. We worked beautifully together. He would lay out a scene, then say, "Dick, you know more about this than I do, so just do it the way you see it, the way you feel it." My costars Lynn Carlin and Linda Lavin were also supportive.

We shot that winter in and around L.A., including at the veterans hospital in Brentwood. There, working amid former servicemen who were dealing with addictions of various types, I was moved by the importance of the story we were trying to tell and decided to go public with my own story, giving Marilyn Beck the exclusive. Her eyes bugged out, too.

Fans were accepting when the news hit. I received thousands of letters. People understood that those who clowned around and made them laugh often had a dark, private side.

The movie aired on February 13, 1974, and both ratings and reaction were strong. AP TV critic Jay Sharbutt's review sounded like a summary of my personal tale. "It's not just a tale about the downfall of a corporate lush," he wrote. "Rather, it's a chilling, sip-by-sip study, stirred with a heavy swizzle stick for dramatic emphasis, of how easily any 'social drinker' can slide into alcoholism without realizing he or she can't handle any kind of drinking."

The "strong and welcome antidote to the usual run of TV movies about happy people with happy problems" earned me an Emmy nomination. Although I lost to Hal Holbrook for his work in another extremely powerful TV movie, *The Pueblo Affair,* I savored the impact of my work. Only the National Association of Alcoholism took exception. They had wanted the ending changed so the guy made it. I argued that the movie would not have had the same impact if it ended happily ever after.

As I knew all too well, the disease did not work that way. Unbeknownst to anyone, on two occasions during production—this was after I had come forward in the press about my alcoholism— I went back to the hotel where I was staying and drank. Both slips were after shooting scenes that, at the end of the day, left me feeling depressed and empty.

After each one, I got sick and swore, Never again, though that promise was easier said than kept.

M argie and I bought a beachfront home on Coronado Island with a spectacular view of the ocean. I also purchased a thirty-three-foot Ranger sloop, which occupied so much of my time that I referred to it as my mistress. From the moment I hoisted my first sail the boat became my escape. I loved being on the water, feeling the sun, the wind, and the salt, and most of all the freedom. It released everything in me that I couldn't otherwise express.

I sailed every day, sometimes up the coast, sometimes straight out into the ocean. I studied navigation, the weather, and ocean currents. I was always on the lookout for something, something I couldn't find.

For a while, I talked of journeying to Fiji—not to live. The commute was too far. "But I'd like to try the lifestyle," I said jokingly.

The entire family was trying out lifestyles. One day when Margie and I were on Coronado, our eldest son called. After graduating from law school, Chris had moved to Salem, Oregon, gotten married, and most recently made us grandparents with the birth of his daughter, Jessica. Now he wanted to plant roots. He had his heart set on a one-hundred-year-old home and asked if I'd loan him the money for a down payment.

"Sure," I said. "No problem."

That same afternoon we got a call from our other son, Barry, a great-looking young man who had married a beautiful girl he met when both of them were ushering at a theater. He had also found a house and wanted to borrow money to put down.

Again I said sure, no problem. But then I turned to Margie and said, "We aren't answering the phone the rest of the day."

A short time later Stacy moved to San Francisco with her trumpet-player boyfriend, who used to sit in our living room watching *Kung Fu* and muttering, "Heavy duty." Margie and I constantly rolled our eyes. What did that mean? We did our best to savor the relatively simple concerns of our baby, Carrie Beth, whose big worries, at fourteen, were homework and the prom. I marveled at the equanimity of our fourth-born. By the time she arrived, our attitude as parents was more cavalier than with the first or second, and I think it made Carrie Beth a calmer person. She was an angel of a girl, an old soul with a preternatural ability to read people that made me think she should become a psychologist.

I could have used one. As my children were finding themselves, I was going through the same thing, a sort of adult-onset confusion that had me asking many of the same questions: What was I going to do with my life? What was going to make me happy? Why wasn't I happy?

Like it or not, life is a never-ending confrontation with bouts of uncertainty and chapters of self-discovery. As I was about to learn, it is a series of fine messes that we enter, some wittingly, and others not.

22

ANOTHER FINE MESS

When my daughter Stacy was fourteen, she discovered that she had a beautiful singing voice. We discovered it at the same time.

It was early morning, and my wife and I heard a crystal-clear melodic contralto note sweep through the house, going from room to room and brightening everything along its path. After looking at each other, Margie and I followed the sound into Stacy's bathroom and found her staring at herself in disbelief as she sang that wonderful note.

Singing lessons followed, and in April 1975 I spirited Stacy away from her lazy boyfriend in San Francisco and put her in my latest ABC special, *The Confessions of Dick Van Dyke*. She sang "South Rampart Street" with guest star Michele Lee and me, and then the two of us traded lyrics on "Mockingbird." After that, her voice was no longer a secret and she got involved with musical theater in Scottsdale. But not everything was out in the open.

I followed that special with a pilot for ABC called *MacLeish and the Rented Kid,* a story inspired, I assumed, by the movie *A Thousand Clowns,* as the updated plot felt similar. I played a political cartoonist content with living on my own until I agreed to care for the eleven-year-old son of a war correspondent friend who was sent overseas. I liked the way it came out, but the network had problems with it though they wanted to go forward.

After the frustrations of my last series, though, I was gun-shy about getting into anything that was not perfect and I nixed the series, walking away from my overall deal with the network. While going through that process, I found myself talking about the ups and downs of the business to my agent's secretary, Michelle Triola. I liked her. She was easy to talk to, she understood me, she was interested, and she knew the business.

All the things Margie didn't like, Michelle did, and gradually it got to where I was inventing excuses to call Sol so that I could speak with Michelle. I looked forward to our conversations. Michelle was an opinionated, feisty, smart woman. She wore her dark hair up and large glasses that gave her cute, girlish face a hip sophistication. She was part of the business and liked talking about every aspect of it, especially the people. She seemed to know or have met everyone.

For good reason, too. Michelle had been around. She had studied theater at UCLA before working as a singer and dancer. She was married briefly to actor Skip Ward, best known for his part in *The Night of the Iguana.* Her father took her to Rome to get that marriage annulled. While in Rome, Michelle stumbled upon a jazz festival, introduced herself to the headliner, the great pianist Oscar Peterson, and ended up singing a set with him and his trio, something she talked about for the rest of her life. I would have talked about it, too, had I sung with him.

It was so typical of Michelle. She collected stories the same way she collected friends. She had tons of both. And once touched by her sense of humor and enormous heart, few let go, including her ex, Skip Ward. Later, at the end of his life, he was down on his luck and we supported him. But when I took an interest in Michelle, she was a demi-celebrity on the front pages and in the gossip columns for the drama she was going through in the courts.

At the time, Michelle was suing actor Lee Marvin, with whom she had a six-year relationship between 1964 and 1970. They had met on the movie *Ship of Fools* and begun living together shortly after. She gave up her singing and acting career to be with him, and in turn he promised to support her for the rest of her life. It was as if they were married.

But then he dumped her, leaving Michelle with nothing, and she sued for the same rights a wife would have under California law. Hers was a groundbreaking case that received attention nationwide from all sorts of special-interest groups and individuals. Her attorney, Marvin Mitchelson, who coined the term *palimony,* vowed to take her case to the Supreme Court if necessary, which seemed likely that summer after it was rejected first by California's Superior Court and then by the Second District Court of Appeals.

I provided a friendly ear. When I was in town, I would call the office and end up chatting with her. On occasion, we talked at night or arranged to meet for dinner. Then, when I needed support, I found myself turning to her.

It was that summer, around the time the courts were deciding against Michelle, when Jerry called one day and said our father had turned gravely ill and I needed to get on a plane. This was a day I knew was going to come but wanted desperately to avoid.

My parents had been living with Jerry in Las Vegas for about ten years, ever since my father, at sixty, lost his job at a packing and moving company to a younger man. He was unable to find another one. For the past few months, he had been battling emphysema, the result most likely of forty-plus years of smoking cigarettes. When I arrived at the hospital in Las Vegas, I found both my father and mother sitting in the lobby, crying.

"What's the matter?" I asked, alarmed.

My father could not answer.

"We just saw the doctor," my mother replied between deep breaths. "He said, 'Look, you're an old man. You've got emphysema. You're going to die.'"

"He's going to die?"

She nodded.

I looked over at my father. He was shaking from nerves. Tears were streaming down the sides of his face. Bad news is one thing, but to break it to a person that bluntly and that insensitively was unconscionable.

I flew into a rage and ran around the hospital screaming for the doctor who had examined my father. I was going to beat the shit out of him. I had never been this upset in my entire life. I covered as much of that hospital as I could and never found the doctor. He was either hiding or he had left.

We decided to move my father to a hospital in Phoenix where they specialized in treating emphysema. He was cognizant of everything that was happening, and although he was dying, he was still himself, a charmer and a jokester. As he was carried on a stretcher onboard the chartered plane taking us to Phoenix, he turned to the pilot and flight attendant and in a suave British accent said, "Hello, I'm David Niven."

On the night he died, I was with my mother in a motel near the hospital. Apparently my father's heart began to race and he asked the nurse if she could get it down. She said, "We're working on it, Mr Van Dyke." He passed away a few hours later. We took his body back to Danville for burial. We started out flying on a commercial airline, but on a layover in Dallas I thought, What the heck am I doing? I was distraught and so was my family. So I chartered a plane to take us the rest of the way.

We deplaned at the tiny airport in Danville and stood on the tarmac, tired and unsure what to do next. Jerry put his arm around my shoulder.

"Let's take a cab to the hotel," he said. "It's my treat since you got the jet."

We cracked up and knew my father would have laughed the loudest if he had heard.

There was more shuffling to be done. Soon after, my father-in-law died and we moved my mother and my mother-in-law into a lovely apartment near our place on Coronado. As house-mates, they were the female version of the odd couple. They were either laughing hysterically or fighting. We were constantly mediating one issue or another. Between such real-life details, my nascent feelings for Michelle, and my marriage, I felt I needed to spend a while on the beach figuring out my life.

But suddenly I found myself listening to Bob Einstein and his writing-producing partner, Allan Blye, both veteran writer-producers of the *Smothers Brothers* and *Sonny and Cher* variety shows, pitch me an idea for a variety show. Despite asking myself why the hell I wanted to do a TV series when I could spend all day doing nothing, I heard myself, for reasons I did not want to analyze, say, "Let's try it."

The one-hour special, called *Van Dyke & Company,* aired in October 1975 and featured guest stars Carl Reiner, Gabe Kaplan, Ike and Tina Turner, plus a surprise appearance from Mary Tyler Moore. My young executive producers and their crew of hip writers, including Steve Martin, guided me more in the direction of *Saturday Night Live* than *Your Show of Shows,* and it paid off. Kay Gardella of the New York *Daily News* praised the special as "skillfully crafted" and "fresh and offbeat." Even an admitted non-fan of mine, the *New York Times'* John O'Connor, called it "pleasantly agreeable."

Buoyed by the positive reaction, NBC execs decided to put *Van Dyke & Company* on the fall schedule as a weekly series. The network seemed confident we could find an audience in the heart of the family hour; I was hopeful, but not as sure since we were opposite three popular shows—*The Waltons; Welcome Back, Kotter;* and *Barney Miller.* My manager called that a "suicide" time slot. Then at the last minute we were moved. I wanted to believe this was good news.

"No, it's worse than suicide," Byron said.

"Worse?" I asked. "What could be worse than suicide?"

"Thursdays at ten P.M.," he said. "Nobody is watching a show like yours at that hour."

B ut I was too old to care about ratings. After reassuring Bob and Allan and the rest of the staff that I was not afraid to try anything, we premiered the new season with guests Flip Wilson,

Chevy Chase, Dinah Shore, and Andy Kaufman, one of our staff writers, who played the loser in a Fonzie look-alike skit that was typical Andy. We kept up the zaniness with Carol Burnett, John Denver, Sid Caesar, Tina Turner, and our own staff, including Andy, Pat Proft, Marilyn Sokol, and Bob, who debuted his "Super Dave" character in a bit where he gets sick on a Disneyland roller coaster.

We amused ourselves more than anyone. In the middle of a production number, for instance, Andy wandered onstage, looking like he had just beamed down to the planet from an alien culture. The confused audience laughed nervously as I tried to figure out why he had interrupted my song. Andy just shrugged. I pretended to be upset by the interruption and walked offstage, leaving Andy to stare blankly at the audience. Of course, it was planned—or at least to the degree you could plan anything with Andy.

My young, smart staff of silly, subversive, upstart writers continued to break all the rules of prime-time variety shows. One skit turned TV itself inside out by examining how an imaginary sit-com titled *Honey, I'm Home* would be written for three different time slots, and I acted out each variation. At eight P.M., I walked through the front door and my wife said dinner was nearly ready. At nine P.M., I came home and found her kissing another man. At ten P.M., I came home to another man who was fixing us dinner.

My favorite piece was a sketch we did each week about a family of morons, the Bright Family, and the dumber we made them, the funnier it was. I rarely got through those without busting up. Unfortunately, the jokes were lost on other people and ratings failed to materialize. A move in November to an earlier time slot did not improve the numbers, and the following month NBC canceled the show.

Was I surprised?

No, you can see the writing on the wall when your show is shuffled around in the schedule.

But vindication was just around the corner. *Van Dyke & Company* received three Emmy nominations and then Bob, Allan, and I left the September 1977 gala holding statues we had won for Outstanding Comedy-Variety or Music Series. I couldn't believe we had beaten *The Carol Burnett Show*. Allan couldn't believe we had beaten *Saturday Night Live* and *The Muppets*. Bob shook his head as if the two of us were missing the point and then quipped, "I can't believe we won and we're out of a job."

I feared I might have been out of more than just a job, though, as my risk taking was not confined to the show. I am talking about Michelle. Over the four months we worked on the show, I was drawn into a relationship with her. I was five days in L.A., two on Coronado. Our phone conversations turned into lunches and those evolved into low-key dinners in dark restaurants where we could avoid attention. If anyone had asked, I was ready to explain that Michelle was my agent's secretary and we had met up to sign papers.

But no one asked. Fortunately, no one saw us in the corner of Dan Tana's or any of our other nighttime haunts. Michelle and I would talk throughout the day. She loved show business and wanted to hear about what had happened on the set, the bits that worked and those that did not work, who the guests were, and all that stuff. She had ideas and opinions and understood my ambitions and frustrations.

It was the opposite of Margie, who liked Coronado but loved the isolation of the desert even more. Margie took up painting and weaving and she became quite good at them. I worked harder going back and forth between my two worlds than I did on the show. I lost seven pounds in the first two months. I told people it was the work. In truth, it was the stress of dividing my time between two extremely strong, attractive women.

Margie kept trying to pull me away, out of Hollywood. She wanted us to go somewhere. We had already gone to the desert, then to the beach, but that was not enough. Forget about show business, she said. As far as she was concerned, I had already done Broadway, television, and movies. What more was there to prove? What more was there to do?

But suddenly I was involved with a woman who loved what I did for a living and not only knew all the people in the business, but understood that performing was in my blood, somehow part of my DNA, and that all my talk of retirement was bunk. I wasn't going to stop. I couldn't.

In December, Michelle talked me through the sting of *Van Dyke & Company*'s cancellation and I helped her celebrate when California's Supreme Court ruled in her favor, saying that an agreement to share assets between a nonmarried couple living together was binding. With the holidays upon us, I woke up to what was happening to me, or in reality what *had* happened. I was involved with a woman other than my wife. It was unbelievable. I was writhing in guilt. I had to do something.

23

DIVORCE. AMERICAN STYLE

I n the spring of 1976 I stood alongside fifty prominent figures
from politics, entertainment, sports, and the clergy in front
of the Washington, D.C., press corps and acknowledged that
I was a recovering alcoholic. Astronaut Buzz Aldrin, former baseball pitcher Don Newcombe, Representative Wilbur Mills, and
TV host Garry Moore were among those at the event also helping
to eliminate the stigma and shame that often prevented people
from owning up to the disease.

With all those individuals shedding their anonymity and
sharing personal stories, it was a powerful, well-managed spec-
tacle, and afterward I had dinner with one of the event organizers
and his wife. We ate in their hotel suite, and to my astonishment,
they had a pre-dinner cocktail, opened a bottle of wine, got absolutely smashed, and then fought. I finally excused myself.

I considered going public about their hypocrisy but thought

better of it, and put the unpleasant incident out of my mind. One night, months later, though, actually toward the end of the year, the memory returned with all the subtlety of a car wreck as I sat across from Michelle at dinner, sipping my second martini of the night, and I thought, Oh my God, I am just like them—a hypocrite.

I don't know why I was surprised that I was drinking again. The booze spirited me away from the guilt and unpleasantness I felt for betraying the vows I had taken to be faithful to my wife. I had never cheated on her before. In fact, I had never come close to it. It was just like when I first realized I had a drinking problem. I would be in the shower, driving my car, or sitting in front of the TV and suddenly say to myself, "This can't be happening to me."

The few people I let in on the secret all said the same thing: I was fifty years old and was undergoing a stereotypical midlife crisis. Indeed, I had to consider that a strong possibility. How could I not when I woke up every morning and asked myself, "Am I going in the right direction?"

For fifty years, I never worried about which direction I was headed. I went any way the wind blew. Now, all of a sudden, I had no idea. However, I knew that Michelle and I, despite being opposite personalities—she was a strong-willed force of nature while I was content to stand in the back and smile—got along as if we were meant to be together. As a result, I asked myself how something that felt so right could also feel so wrong.

After much soul-searching and many nerve-racking months, I wanted to get on with my life, and there was only one way to do it. I needed to be honest with Margie. We were on Coronado one day and I told her. I said that there was another woman whom I liked a lot. Margie was terribly shocked, as I had expected, and both of us were confused. We had known each other so long that we could not conceive of a divorce.

After many emotional but productive talks, Margie and I agreed to do what we had basically been doing for years; live our separate lives, or more accurately, live our lives separately. She returned to the desert and I went to my rental in Hollywood. I made sure Margie knew she would never want for anything materially or financially. My one regret was leaving her alone. For myself, I was confident that I was making the right decision.

M y oldest son, Chris, now a deputy district attorney in Salem, had recently gone through his own divorce, and the other children were wiser and more understanding and accepting than I had expected. In April they helped me celebrate the opening of *Same Time Next Year* at the Huntington Hartford Theater in Pasadena. Stacy, twenty-two, noted that she had not seen me onstage since *Bye Bye Birdie,* prompting Carrie Beth, sixteen, to remind all of us that she was not even born then.

I was starring with my pal Carol Burnett. We set new box-office records, some of which were due to the anticipation generated by the announcement that I was joining her long-running variety show. Carol and I had a special chemistry dating back to when we teamed up on the game show *Pantomime Quiz.* Now, nearly thirty years later, we still spurred each other into new realms of silly. In *Same Time Next Year,* instead of taking a bow at the end, she jumped into bed as an old lady and I scrambled after her as an old man with a bottle of Geritol. Then the curtain came down. Even though the playwright, Bernard Slade, disapproved of the way we hammed it up, the audience screamed. On closing night, we took it a step further. After I got into bed, Tim Conway shuffled across the stage dressed as a butler and holding a tray with a bottle of champagne. People laughed for an hour.

Carol's and my partnership had been rekindled when she came on *Van Dyke & Company*. We had pantomimed a fight at the end of a skit that ended up with the two of us rolling on the ground in slow motion as we traded punches and kicks. It was such fun that she suggested we do a show together. Instead of that happening, we did the play, and then Harvey Korman left *The Carol Burnett Show* after ten years and suddenly I found myself replacing a multitalented actor who was also the world's greatest second banana.

But Harvey proved irreplaceable. Despite the fanfare in the press as the new season began in September, I was uncomfortable in the skits and unable to find a rhythm among a cast that had been together for a decade. It must have been the same for actors who came on to *The Dick Van Dyke Show*. Even though we were welcoming, we had our own ways of communicating that resulted from having been together every day for years.

Carol and the others did everything they could to help me, but the writers were still producing sketches with Harvey in mind and I could not on my own figure out where I fit in. At the end of September, I told the AP's Jerry Buck that my timing was getting better. Tim also offered encouraging words. Privately, though, he came to my dressing room and commiserated.

Finally, at the end of November, I called off the experiment. My final show was December 3, 1977. I blamed it on the difficult commute between Arizona and L.A., saying I spent too many hours in the airport or on the road and too few with my family. Carol's executive-producer husband, Joe Hamilton, released a statement saying they hated to lose me. In the end, it was sad but a nice try and quite simply not my cup of tea.

I n late spring 1978, Stanley Kramer, the Oscar-winning director
responsible for such classic films as *Guess Who's Coming to
Dinner, Inherit the Wind,* and *Judgment at Nuremberg,* took me
to lunch at the Brown Derby, a landmark Hollywood watering
hole, and put a copy of the script for his next movie, which he was
directing and producing, on the table. Based on the dramatic 1976
Broadway play, *The Runner Stumbles* was a strong, complicated
look at a priest in a small mining town who falls in love with
a young nun. Stanley had already cast Kathleen Quinlan as the
nun, and he wanted me as the priest.

I had read the script several times prior to lunch and related
more than Stanley knew to the mysterious forces that weighed on
the priest. But I wanted to pass.

"It's out of my reach," I said. "This is heavy drama and I fear
that I'll embarrass all of us."

Stanley ordered dessert and kept on me about the role. That
summer, after he agreed to take full responsibility if the film
bombed, I let him talk me into a deal and started work on the picture. Along with Kathleen, Maureen Stapleton, and Beau Bridges,
we shot in Roslyn, Washington, a rural little town that oozed
charm and was full of warm locals who took lots of photos, asked
for autographs, and went slack-jawed this one memorable day
when they overheard me greet Maureen, who was poised on the
steps of her dressing-room trailer with a little bottle in her hand.

"Where the hell are you off to?" she asked.

"Getting a cup of coffee," I said. "Do you want anything?"

"I want you to come in here and fool around with me,"
she said.

I turned white, as did those standing nearby.

"Consider it a mercy mission," she said.

"Can I get you anything else?" I said, laughing nervously while continuing to walk briskly away.

There were few other highlights. Stanley was a marvelous producer, but he did not do much as a director beyond telling me that he didn't want to see "a vestige of Dick Van Dyke, not a word, not a body movement." Then why cast me? He made me so self-conscious that I couldn't get into a single scene. I was lost. At night I brooded and read the Bible and Carl Jung's *Modern Man in Search of a Soul,* looking for thoughts and information that might help me reach more of an understanding of the role.

The superb actors around me also tried to help, and Kathleen, a serious actress who knew her business, felt so sorry for me. She knew I was trying and gave me everything she could. But I could not get a hold of the part. Today I could do it. Back then I was not ready.

In my early fifties, I was going through a phase where few things felt right and I was trying to figure out those that did. It was not uncommon. In your twenties, you pursue your dreams. By your late thirties and early forties, you hit a certain stride. Then you hit your fifties, you get your first annoying thoughts of mortality, you begin more serious questioning of not just the meaning of your life but of what's working, what's not working, and what you still want, and all of a sudden you don't know which way is up. You thought you knew but don't. You just want to get to where life feels okay again.

For me, that meant returning to the stage, the place where I found the most satisfaction: I agreed to star in Lawrence Roman's play *Tragedies/A Comedy,* a play that resonated with me for many reasons. It was, as I told a *New York Times* reporter writing about the upcoming theater season, "about a man's midlife emotional crisis. The character I play is confused. He realizes there's not much time left and panics. He and his wife separate, and he runs into an old girlfriend and tries to recapture what he had with her in his salad days."

I was intrigued with the effect the play would have on me, mining that territory night after night. But I did not get the chance to see. The financing fell through following a production delay and I snapped up the lead in a revival of *The Music Man*, the beloved story of softhearted con man Harold Hill, which Robert Preston made into one of Broadway's hottest tickets in 1957.

I had always loved the play and they offered a decent weekly salary plus a sizable cut of the box office. Broadway veteran Michael Kidd, whose credits included *Guys and Dolls* and *Finian's Rainbow*, directed and choreographed, and we had a show-stopper in Christian Slater, then a twelve-year-old boy, who sang "Gary, Indiana" with an enthusiasm that made people take note. I could tell he was going to be something.

We opened with a nine-week run in Reno, Nevada, and I went up early to acclimate myself to the altitude. I was not too worried about losing my breath mid-song, but hey, I was going on tour and I was a grandfather—now three times over, thanks to Barry and his wife; Stacy, twenty-five, married, and performing a nightclub act with her husband in Phoenix, was about to add a fourth to the next generation of Van Dykes.

Other family considerations were on my mind, too. While I was doing the play, Margie booked herself on an around-the-world cruise, an adventure lasting several months. Like me, she wanted to get away and think about her life, and with Carrie Beth now eighteen and in junior college, she could finally do so without worry. The long break worked for both of us. In February 1980, as the play debuted in Los Angeles, Margie was arriving in China. I mentioned her adventure to reporters who asked about my marriage, but gave the impression that ours was the same, stable union as always.

In many ways, it was.

Meanwhile, Michelle, who the year before had won a $104,000 judgment against Lee Marvin but lost her $3.6 million community-property argument, kept me company as often as her job permitted. She had been in Reno for the play's opening, kept a regular but low profile at the Pantages Theater, where we played in Hollywood, and visited me when we took the play to San Francisco. With her encouragement, I looked up my first leading lady, Fran Adams, whom I'd worked with in TV back in Atlanta. Now she was Fran Kearton, a successful Bay Area artist.

As we reminisced about our silly *Fran and Dick Show,* Fran reminded me of the time we'd booked Helen Hayes. Both Fran and I had been extremely nervous about the fabled first lady of Broadway visiting our humble local show. We rehearsed tirelessly and spruced up our studio with flowers.

Then Helen arrived, admittedly and apologetically jittery. She explained that it was because she had never seen herself on TV. Thinking I would put her at ease, I said, "Don't worry. You don't look half as bad as you think."

I think it took me a couple weeks before I could pull my foot all the way out of my mouth.

Reviews of the play were mixed, with most of the negative comments similar to those of the *New York Times'* Walter Kerr, who declared me not enough of a scoundrel. "Mr. Van Dyke isn't a dirty rotten crook," he wrote. "He's not even a natty gentleman crook. He's not a crook at all. He's a nimble performer, and an attractive one, and before the play is over he is able to bring into the play a good bit of the lively shtick he's perfected over the years . . . [but] he is simply—and only—nice."

Not according to some. After the play, I was the recipient of an atypical amount of bad press. There were small, nasty items and asides in features. They were like paper cuts, lots of little annoying cuts. I couldn't figure out why. I guessed for some reason various writers decided that I was, at nearly fifty-five years old, fair game, and therefore eligible to be called temperamental and bitter.

I wasn't any of that, though I was clearly something. What that was, I didn't know. I had hoped Margie would return from her voyage with a fresh perspective, but she was not in any hurry to divorce.

I didn't argue, and when our son, Chris, was sworn in as district attorney of Marion County in September 1980, the two of us stood side by side in Salem's city hall, beaming like parents who had never been prouder, which was true. With a few minor contributions from Carl Reiner, Mary Tyler Moore, and Carol Burnett, Chris got himself elected by running a grassroots campaign emphasizing character, honesty, and dedication to the law. Most people never knew he had a famous father until I showed up for the swearing-in.

I wasn't surprised. In high school, Chris played on the football team. One day after practice, as he and some of his teammates were cleaning up the equipment, a kid suddenly hit him in the nose. Blood was everywhere. When Chris asked why he did that, the kid said, "I wanted to see if a Van Dyke would bleed." It was senseless.

I met him in the emergency room at the hospital. After I heard what had happened, I was livid. I wanted to know the kid's name. But Chris refused to tell me. He said, "Dad, he's from a dysfunctional family. He's really screwed up." Chris was well into his term as the DA before he finally told me, and even then he still made me promise not to track the guy down.

Of course, he was joking. But that's the way he was.

He once accompanied a group of police officers on a drug raid in the country. As they snuck up on the house, they came upon a dead hog lying in the thick grass. Chris muttered, "Officer down," and it nearly blew the operation as they all laughed. But he was tough. A year after he was elected, he won his biggest case, convicting a serial killer known as the I-5 Murderer.

In August 1981, the truth about my marriage began to leak out. A showbiz gossip column ran this item: "Just watch Dick Van Dyke finally get a divorce from his wife, Margie, and marry his longtime friend, Michelle Triola Marvin (of Lee Marvin palimony fame)." The reality that the public was now privy to my long-kept secret jarred me.

At the time, I was talking on and off to a therapist. I had started seeing her about my drinking, which I had convinced myself was due to emotional problems, not alcoholism. She quickly disabused me of that notion, though, and said flat out that I had a disease. As far as emotional problems, she got me to confront the obvious, the real reason I had started to see her: my marriage. As she said, I was caught between two strong women, and like it or not, I had to make a choice or else I would continue to torture myself.

The choice was almost made for me in August when the California State Court of Appeals ruled that Lee Marvin did not have to pay Michelle the $104,000 judgment handed down two years earlier. She was extremely upset. After years of fighting a fight that would affect numerous women but doing it very much alone, Michelle saw the only victory she had won taken away from her. I felt terrible for her and gave her the money. But that irked Margie. In fact, it was the last straw.

It seemed that Margie, despite all that we had talked about, held on to a thread of hope that I might return to our marriage, go back to the desert or wherever we might live. But when I said it was my half of our money to do with what I wanted, including give it to Michelle, she knew it was over.

And it was. Even though it took us another three years to finalize the divorce, our marriage was, at that point, officially through. Though Margie was angry—she feared I was leaving the family for another, separate life—our split was still amicable. I made sure she knew that she could have anything she wanted, everything she thought she might need for her comfort and security, and as time passed she saw that I was not abandoning anyone.

In many ways, we became better friends. No longer constrained by a marriage that was not working, we could accept that we had grown apart and instead focus on growing up. Both of us started over. There was nothing wrong with that.

In fact, it felt good. It was time.

24

EM-VA-ZEMA

I once told my children that if not for them, I probably would have ended up on the streets because I did not have any strong ambition pushing me to earn a living. So I could not have been any happier when I found myself not having to worry about supporting my children or even earning a living. The slow lane fit me like one of my custom-made suits. Michelle and I, tired of shuttling between our separate residences, got a condo together in Marina del Rey, and we whiled away afternoons on a new sailboat.

We sailed every day we could. One day we were on the ocean when a storm kicked up and the water turned rough. Ordinarily I handled all the sailing chores myself while she enjoyed the sun, but this time, needing her help, I began barking orders. I sounded very much like a captain as I told her to take the line portside, wait for me to come about, and then move starboard.

Instead of jumping into action, as a good first mate would, Michelle stood still, glaring at me as if I was speaking to her in gibberish.

"What's wrong?" I asked.

"Never mind the bullshit nautical terms," she said. "Just tell me right or left."

I cracked up and continued to laugh all the way back to the dock. I loved her, and the life we were living together. This was not a new me as much as it was the lazier version of the me that I had always imagined—carefree, suntanned, waking up without a plan, enjoying life. I got offered sitcoms but none that grabbed me. I stayed involved by hosting the annual People's Choice Awards and starring in Showtime's remake of *The Country Girl,* the Clifford Odets play about an alcoholic actor and his wife.

It's hard to imagine now, but at the end of 1981 and in early 1982, cable was new, premium channels like HBO and Showtime even newer. I wanted to be a part of the cutting-edge material they were putting on TV. When I started in TV you couldn't even say the word *pregnant.*

I had high hopes for the gritty picture. It had earned Uta Hagen a Tony in 1950 and Grace Kelly an Oscar for the 1954 movie version. I would be stepping into the role Bing Crosby had played, and I thought Blythe Danner, whom I adored and had talked to over the years about working together, would play my wife. But I got to New York, where we were shooting, and learned I had a different leading lady, Faye Dunaway.

I would not have done the picture if I had known in advance. Nothing against Faye, but I wanted to work with Blythe. I understood the reasons for the change. Faye was a bigger name, and the producers assumed that would draw more viewers. As it affected me, well, Faye was a much different kind of actress than Blythe. Perhaps it was the project. She could have been concerned about reprising a role that two great actresses had already performed, which would have been understandable; I had my own issues about comparisons to Bing, something I did not ordinarily worry about.

But Faye was high strung, a handful as they say, and this cast a certain pall over the project. One day she ordered Michelle off the set, explaining that she did not want anyone in her line of sight. I liked Michelle on the set; she gave me excellent notes. After we wrapped, Faye insisted on reshooting a scene that I thought was my best dramatic work ever. Michelle speculated that might have been the reason for the reshoot.

When all was finally done, I had one question: Where were the comedies?

Drama was fine, but my first love was making people laugh.

I had long talks with Michelle about the changing state of comedy. Comedy was a world where the ground shifted every couple of years. New people arrived and the veterans moved to the side, but they did not disappear. Funny was funny. It would always be in demand. People seemed to need to laugh as much as they needed anything else. Did it matter, she asked, if I never found another sitcom?

Her question was not an invitation to quit looking for the right project as much as it was a stake she hammered into the ground to mark a point in time, that being the end of my midlife crisis. I did not have to try to compete with anything I had done in the past, she said. Critics would always make comparisons to *The Dick Van Dyke Show*, but that was their job, not mine.

My job was to continue to be me and answer only to the voice inside me that knew whether something felt right.

I gladly said yes to a hodgepodge of TV movies, starting with

Drop-Out Father, a satire that let me make light of a man going through a midlife crisis. Costarring with Mariette Hartley, I played an advertising executive who looks at his Greenwich, Connecticut, life and sees nothing worthwhile, nothing of substance and meaning. He reacts by locking himself in his bedroom for eleven days and reading *War and Peace* from start to finish.

After that accomplishment, he rejoins his family with a determination to drop out and start fresh. He quits his job and destroys his family's credit cards. Today the movie's references to the book *Passages* and to group therapy give it the feel of a time capsule. But it was a fun romp that made a few good points about something a lot of us were going through, and it was NBC's highest-rated movie of the season.

A few months later, I partnered with Sid Caesar on the movie *Found Money,* directed by Bill Persky. Sid and I played a couple of guys at a bank who have lost their jobs to computers, but my character, a computer expert, figures out a way to turn the tables by using a computer to withdraw money from the bank's dormant accounts and give it to deserving people. I hoped this latter-day Robin Hood tale might get turned into a series. It didn't.

My favorite role, though, was off-screen: watching my kids. Actually, I no longer had children. I had four grown-ups. By the time *Found Money* aired toward the end of 1983, Chris was finishing up his term as DA, planning a new career with Nike, and getting remarried. Barry was acting in numerous pilots, Stacy had gotten divorced, and Carrie Beth got married.

In 1984 my divorce was also finalized under amicable terms and afterward Michelle and I left for a two-week sailing adventure in the British Virgin Islands. We got a forty-foot boat, threw a bunch of groceries on it, and took off all by ourselves. It would always remain our favorite vacation together ever. We put down anchor in uninhabited coves, Michelle cooked dinner, and we watched the sun set while the waves and the tropical air lulled us to sleep.

One day we found an island called Jost Van Dyke. We stayed there overnight and learned that a Dutch pirate had named the island after himself. A local rowed out to our boat and tried selling us seashell jewelry he had made. I told him that my name was Van Dyke. He was not impressed.

"Everybody on the island is named Van Dyke," he said.

The solitude was a strange and wonderful experience. We were getting used to it when we pulled into a little island one night at sunset. I saw one other boat out a ways from where we dropped anchor. As we ate dinner, I said, "Man, this is getting away." But a short while later, the silence was broken by the gentle sound of the guy from the other boat rowing toward us in his dinghy. When he got close, he said, "Are you Van Dyke?"

"Yes," I said.

"I have a message," he said. "Your agent is trying to reach you."

He had gone on channel 16 on the shortwave radio and found me. I took a boat back to Tortola, then caught a bus into town, where I picked up a script he had FedExed. It stank. Before I left town, though, I saw a gorgeous home on the water and inquired with a local Realtor about its availability. He called me back ten years later and said it was for sale.

I passed. It was too late. Real estate is mostly about location, but like so many other things in life, it's also about timing.

Cloris Leachman is a gifted actress, but she is an even more outstanding character away from the camera. I don't recommend smoking cigarettes around her, though, as I did when we worked on the movie *Breakfast with Les and Bess*. Based on Lee Kalcheim's off-Broadway play about a husband and wife who host a radio talk show from their apartment near Central Park, the film shot in Toronto, and almost from the time Michelle and I arrived, Cloris was on my case about the way I ate, drank, and of course *smoked*.

"I'm trying to quit," I told her.

"What's the problem?" she asked testily.

"I'm addicted," I said.

She grabbed my cigarettes and tossed them into the trash.

"There goes your addiction," she said.

If only it had been that easy. Our dressing rooms were at opposite ends of the building where we shot, but if I lit up, I would hear her scream from down the hallway, "I smell cigarette smoke." Moments later, whether she was dressed or wearing a robe, she stomped into my dressing room and took the cigarette out of my mouth. When we had lunch together, she ordered for me. One day she told the waiter to bring me a baked potato, no butter, stuffed with vegetables. Another time she picked out all the croutons from my salad.

"The croutons, too?" I asked.

"They're bad for you," she said.

I never got to eat anything I wanted. Michelle, who had known Cloris for years, was thoroughly amused, and since she smoked, too, the two of us frequently found ourselves hiding from her. We felt like a couple of teenagers sneaking a smoke. You had to have a sense of humor around Cloris. She was a very free spirit, with many quirks, all of them endearing once you dialed in to her frequency.

She was also one of those actresses who worked from "business"—carefully contrived mannerisms intended to bring her character more fully alive. In other words, she made a life for her character, from the inside out, and worked off that palette of traits and idiosyncrasies. If her character liked tea, she'd want to make tea, then drink it in a scene. She added fifty little things that weren't in the script. She drove the director out of his gourd; at one point he threatened to walk off the set, exclaiming, "I can't take it anymore."

But eventually he calmed down and understood, and you know what? Cloris was right. An actor has to do something as she stands there and talks. Her character needs a life. Cloris understood that, had her method, and that's what made her so good.

Later, Cloris was happy to hear that I had given up cigarettes. I did not tell her why. I did not want to hear her say, I told you so. She would have had every right to say it, too.

Our movie aired in April 1985, but about six months before, I'd suddenly developed a problem in my neck—actually, a spur that caused pain in my arm. I had to undergo a minor operation. Prior to surgery, I went into St. John's Hospital in Santa Monica for X-rays. As I left, a radiologist stopped me. A small, slight man from India, he spoke with a mellifluous accent that made his invitation to step back into the examining room sound almost benign.

But it wasn't.

"Do you see those spots?" he asked after putting my X-rays against a light panel so I could see my lungs.

"Yes," I said.

"Em-va-zema," he said.

"What?" I asked.

"These are spots from em-va-zema."

He shook his head as if it was weighted with the melancholy of a future only he could see. But I could see it, too. I pictured my father lying in his hospital bed, breathing through a tube as a result of em-va-zema.

"What?" I asked.

"I don't want to lose you, Mr. Van Dyke," he said. "You must stop the smoking."

"I will," I said.

And I did. After walking out of the hospital, I bought the patch and started chewing nicotine gum, and I have not smoked a cigarette since. That doctor's prescience probably saved my life.

25

STRONG MEDICINE

Booze was the next thing to go.

It wasn't like I had a checklist, though. Despite all the effort I'd devoted to giving up alcohol in the past, despite programs I tried and the promises I'd made to myself, sobriety just happened as I was living my life.

In the fall of 1985, I made *Strong Medicine,* a TV miniseries based on Arthur Hailey's novel about the pharmaceutical industry. We shot in London with a cast that included *Dallas*'s Patrick Duffy and Pamela Sue Martin, and also Sam Neill, Ben Cross, Annette O'Toole, and Douglas Fairbanks Jr., who, at eighty-five, provided a debonair air of fun by coming to the set every day dressed to the nines and hitting on all the actresses.

I hadn't worked there since I made *Chitty Chitty Bang Bang,* but the city and the countryside charmed me all over again. Michelle and I settled in a hotel around the corner from Hyde

Park. She redid our room, made friends with the hotel staff, and eventually convinced them to redesign their restaurant's menus. Basically, she took over the hotel and we were treated like royalty.

During downtime on the set, I indulged my interest in poetry, as well as reciting poetry out loud, and poor Michelle had to sit and listen to me recite verse in an English accent, which, I have to say, had improved since I first tried it out in *Mary Poppins*. As long as I was around people who spoke with an English accent, mine was more than passable. For a while, I entertained the idea of moving there, to a little place in the hills of Broadway, also known as the "Jewel of the Cotswolds," and if not for the tax structure there we might've actually moved.

I don't know whether it was because I was so relaxed in England and comfortable within my life or whether something in my body chemistry changed, but all of a sudden I lost both my taste and tolerance for alcohol. It first happened in England and continued after we returned to L.A. Instead of giving me a lift, a cocktail or glass of wine made me sick to my stomach.

Michelle still enjoyed a cocktail or two, and if we went to a party she'd get silly with the rest of them, but I began to pass. We were making dinner at home one night and after taking a sip of wine I put the glass down and said, "Boy, that's making me ill." From then on, I lost my desire to drink. Finally, I just stopped trying altogether and then I lost the taste altogether.

After a certain point, I never hid the fact that I had a drinking problem. I may not have been open about the long struggle I endured in giving it up completely, but once it happened I never wanted a drink again. Over the years, people would ask how I stopped and I would shrug, as mystified and curious as anyone. It was as if my body did what my mind couldn't: It said, "Enough!"

Sometimes I wonder if I no longer needed it, if the intricate

complications within me somehow, finally, straightened themselves out.

At sixty-one, I was happy and content in my life—and with
myself. There were no more internal fires to put out. The con-
flicts I had battled for years had been resolved. Good decisions
had prevailed, and time had proven the strongest medicine. Margie had moved to a lovely house on the Oregon coast. The kids
were all doing well, and so were the grandchildren.

Now a decade into our relationship, Michelle and I bought
a Spanish-style hacienda in Malibu. We wanted to get married,
something we never got around to doing even though it was
always on our to-do list. We were either too busy sailing, relaxing at home, or visiting with friends, and time flew by. As friends
such as Richard Deacon and Jerry Paris passed away, I counted
my blessings. I wanted another series. I read numerous scripts
and treatments, but nothing resonated in a way that motivated me
to give up my life of leisure.

It made me appreciate even more the once-in-a-lifetime
opportunity that had come my way back when Carl Reiner sent
me not a treatment or a script but eight completed scripts for a
new series—and they were all brilliant in every way. What had
changed since then? Were there fewer geniuses? Was it the business? Or were expectations off? Did every decade have only a few
gems that would stand the test of time, and those of us who were
part of them simply have to thank our lucky stars?

George C. Scott lived near us for a while and the two of us
wanted to do a series together. We came up with an idea
that would have us playing two retired attorneys who opened a
tiny law office and did pro bono work, except we were on opposite

sides of the political fence. He would be the conservative who helped tax cheats and white-collar criminals, and I was the liberal with the bleeding heart. We thought it would be great, but we could not get anyone at the networks to bite.

Instead, I made the rounds as a guest star on other series, starting with Andy Griffith's show *Matlock.* For years, Andy had periodically checked in from his North Carolina home and said, "Let's do something." For this first and only time we actually did. I played the bad guy, the judge in a murder trial who turned out to be the murderer.

Next was *Highway to Heaven* with Michael Landon, who ran the perfect company, since practically all of his crew started with him on *Bonanza.* They were like an extended family. I played a homeless guy who had a little puppet show on skid row. It was perfect for me: dressing up like an old man, entertaining kids. I think it was one of my best performances ever. But my favorite moment was off-camera.

We shot late at night on skid row in downtown L.A., and during a break I took a walk slightly beyond the production and the cops who were protecting us. I wanted to stay in character for the next scene. I sat on the curb and placed my props—a brown sack of puppets and a bottle—next to me. Soon a couple of real-life homeless guys sat down and asked if I would share my drink.

"It's—" I was going to explain that it was not booze, that it was actually a prop. Then I thought better of it.

"Here, take it," I said, after which I walked away so I would not be there when they realized it was tea.

I got another dose of the streets when I worked with comedian and *Sanford and Son* star Redd Foxx on the TV movie *Ghost of a Chance.* I played a detective who misfires his gun while chasing a drug dealer in a nightclub and accidentally kills the club's piano player. Naturally, the musician comes back and haunts him—but with the charge to turn both of their lives around. Some network executives saw it as a possible series. We would not have survived twenty-six episodes. The one was dangerous enough.

On the set, Redd fueled his funny bone with Grand Marnier and cocaine. Always high, he was volatile and unpredictable. You never knew what might set him off. One day, he thought he over-heard the director make a racial slur. The director had said the word "boy," as in "boy oh boy," while speaking to a black guy on the crew, but it was not a slur.

Only Redd heard it that way. But that was enough to incite him. First he glared at the director. Then he pulled a large knife out from a sheath in his pant leg and said, "I'm going to cut him up."

Taking him at his word, I moved quickly to head off any bloodshed that wasn't fake by wrapping my arms around Redd and physically restraining him until I was able to convince him that he had misheard things. It was the most tension I had ever experienced on a set and the first physical altercation I'd been involved in since kindergarten.

At the end of March 1987, I flew up to Vancouver to work with my son Barry on the series *Airwolf.* The show, starring Jan-Michael Vincent, Ernest Borgnine, and Alex Cord, had been can-celed by CBS after three years, but the USA network picked it up for a smaller-budgeted fourth season. They moved production to Canada, recycled helicopter shots from old footage, and recast the show with Barry, Geraint Wyn Davies, Michele Scarabelli, and Anthony Sherwood. I was cast in an episode as a mad scien-tist, and we were finishing up work when tragedy struck the fam-ily some 2,500 miles away.

My son Chris's thirteen-year-old daughter, Jessica, was at home in suburban Cleveland, Ohio, where she lived with her mother. She was fighting a mild fever brought on by chicken pox. Feeling crummy, she took four baby aspirins. I'm sure she thought she was helping herself. Instead, by taking those aspirin, she inadvertently triggered a fatal infection that went straight to her liver and brain. Three days later, she fell violently ill and was rushed to the hospital, where exactly a week after taking the aspirin, she died, the result of a rare disease known as Reye's syndrome.

First reported in 1963, Reye's was and still is a medical mystery whose cause is largely unknown but connected to people—mostly children—who take aspirin when they have viral infections like the flu or chicken pox. At the time, there were warnings in small print on most but not all bottles of aspirin. "God knows," Jessica's stepfather told the L.A. Times, "we never knew about Reye's syndrome." None of us did.

But it changed all of our lives forever. Chris came in from Annapolis, where he was a lobbyist for Nike. By the time I jetted back east from Vancouver, Jessica was gone. The loss destroyed everyone—Chris, Jessica's mom, her stepfather, me, Michelle, Margie, the whole family, and countless others in her school and community who knew her.

My first grandchild was a bright, vibrant girl just coming into her own. She played sports, liked the outdoors, and wrote poetry. Always precocious, Jessica had been putting her thoughts on paper for years. Her feelings reflected an old soul, someone concerned with the big, more profound issues of love and death and the relative brevity of life. "A special girl," her parents said of her—and indeed, that was true of the eleven-year-old who wrote this poem titled "Dreams":

All is white,
Objects floating everywhere,
People sleepwalking through life,
Stopping, picking up reality, walking on.
Suddenly a flash,
Out of a dreamworld into reality;
Nothing can last forever.
Only some people never see the flash.

My mind drifted back to a day a year or two earlier when she'd been staying with Chris and his wife, Christine, on the boat where they lived in Annapolis. Both of them had gone to work and left me to watch Jessica. She was all questions, nonstop questions about life, religion, our family history, the universe, everything. She kept me talking all day. It was one of the best and most challenging conversations of my life.

That night, I took her out to dinner and she was absolutely fascinated that everyone knew me. All night long people asked for autographs or said they had enjoyed my work, and each time Jessica looked at me with wide eyes, trying to figure out what was going on. She couldn't believe it.

"Are you special, Grandpa?" she asked.

"No more or less than anyone else," I said.

"Can I be like that someday?" she asked.

"You already are," I said.

Time lessened the immediate pain of losing Jessica, but there was no getting over the loss of someone with so much potential at such a young age. I could not begin to count how many times I asked myself "Why?" The poets have talked about sorrow reminding us of the stuff that matters in our life, but still, why? Why a child? I returned to the many theologians and philosophers I had read, brilliant people who had explored the existence of God, His will, and the meaning of life. Had they said anything about the meaning of life in the aftermath of such a shattering experience?

As near as I could figure, no one had ever said anything on the subject better than Jessica herself. I got out her poems, a little book she put together called *Collected Poems,* which I had saved for years, and I reread the verse that had flowed from her heart. I saw that she got it, she understood, she knew that life was love.

> *Loving each other forever,*
> *Orchestras of heart-beats,*
> *Visits to paradise—*
> *Every word is a kiss.*

PART FOUR

Everybody wants to laugh—
you know that.
They need to laugh. . . .
People need to laugh.

—**Carl Reiner**

✦

26

THE OLD MAN
AND THE TV

For years, Michelle was a holdout smoker. Long after I gave up cigarettes, long after almost everyone we knew gave up the cancer sticks, she continued to puff away. Her big concession to all the health warnings was to give up her preferred brand of unfiltered smokes, though she continued to purchase stronger brands while turning a deaf ear to my harangues to take better care of herself. Once, I even caught her smoking in the shower.

But then she got a message she couldn't ignore.

While out shopping one day, she was carrying an armload of clothes when suddenly she felt a sharp pain in her chest and lost her breath. Scared, she dropped everything and drove to the CBS studio where I was working on a new sitcom for the network's 1988 fall lineup. I took one look at her and somehow knew she was having, or had just had, a heart attack.

I laid her down in my dressing room and made sure she was comfortable while Grant Tinker, who, though no longer Mary's husband, still ran their MTM production company, called an ambulance. Michelle chewed both of us out. She didn't want the attention, and she made it abundantly clear that she didn't want to go to the hospital. The paramedics, in turn, made it abundantly clear that she didn't have a choice in the matter.

A few hours later, she was in surgery, undergoing a bypass procedure. It all went well, she recovered, and after a few days Michelle was allowed to go home. And guess what? She never smoked again.

"Just like that?" I asked her.

"I have no idea why, but the craving is gone," she said.

"Just like that?" I asked again.

"Just like that," she said.

Later, as she put more thought into it, Michelle attributed the change to a Jamaican nurse who came into her hospital room and said soothing, perhaps magical things to her as she fluttered in and out of the netherworld between consciousness and painkillers.

"I think that nurse did some island magic," she said.

One thing Michelle did not lose was her sense of humor.

Not long afterward, but long enough that Michelle seemed fully recovered from her surgery, I brought her a cup of coffee in bed. It was morning, and as I set the cup on her nightstand I noticed she was puzzling over the TV remote control in her hand as if she'd never seen it before. She looked up at me.

"What does this do?" she asked.

"I beg your pardon?" I said.

"What does this do?" she asked again.

I thought, Oh Jesus, something odd is going on—and it was. All of a sudden she lost the ability to speak coherently. It appeared she couldn't focus properly. I could see her struggling to capture her thoughts. Quickly, I picked up the front page of the newspaper and asked if she knew what the headline said. She looked at it for a moment, then back up at me and shook her head no.

I threw her into the car and rushed her to St. John's. Within twenty minutes, a doctor was examining her. He took her vitals, checked her heart, then did a neurological workup that included simple questions, such as asking her to name the president of the United States.

It was as if she could see it was Ronald Reagan, but couldn't translate the picture into words.

"I don't know," she said. "But he's an asshole."

According to the doctor Michelle had suffered a transient ischemic attack—a kind of warning stroke whose symptoms would pass within twenty-four hours. And thank God the symptoms did pass and she became herself again, otherwise I might have spent much of my dotage playing nurse.

Once she was given the all-clear sign, though, I returned to work on *The Van Dyke Show,* a new series I agreed to do only in order to enjoy the pleasure of working with my son Barry, who was cast as my on-screen son. Interestingly, that fall, Mary Tyler Moore also had a new series, *Annie McGuire,* and the two of us were scheduled back-to-back in the same hour on CBS.

The network very cleverly announced we were "together" for the first time since the old days. We weren't really together, of course, but it made for a nice, albeit contrived, reunion story. At the annual press tour, where we both promoted our shows, we traded fun, light banter in front of reporters. When someone asked if we'd remained friendly, Mary said she had "true affection and respect for me," but cracked, " [Dick] never really liked me."

Even I laughed at that one.

As for our series, both of us could've used a little more laughter. Mary's show fared better than mine, which was, to put it kindly, a total disaster. The audience didn't buy the premise, which featured me as a retired song-and-dance man who helps his son try to make a go of a fledgling theater in small-town Pennsylvania. Nor did I really buy the premise. And frankly, I don't think the show's writers bought it, either.

C oming off that experience, it was easy for me to say no to Warren Beatty. I said it quite clearly, in fact.

"No."

But Warren has a hearing problem. Like many successful visionaries he hears only what he wants to hear. So when I told him that I had read the part he had in mind for me in his script for *Dick Tracy,* which he had sent over, and did not think I could do anything with it, he said, "Oh Jesus, you're leaving me up in the air."

Mind you, I had never committed. I had yet to even talk to him since he'd messengered the script to the house.

"But—"

"You can't do this to me," he said.

Later I realized that he had already cast the part in his head. It was a fait accompli. He had already cast his girlfriend at the time, Madonna, and pals such as Al Pacino and Dustin Hoffman. I was on his list, too, and what I eventually realized was that whether or not I liked it or even agreed, I was going to be in the movie.

Indeed, the most remarkable thing was that though I had no intention of saying yes, I ended up in the movie anyway, playing the district attorney, D.A. Fletcher.

I spent only three days working on the film, and it was still a strange experience. I had one scene where we were shooting in a small hotel room and I had to fall between a little nightstand and an iron cot. We did six takes and on the last one I hit my shoulder on the iron and it tore my clavicle loose. I took my coat off and the bone was sticking straight up. A doctor was called in and taped me up so I could continue work.

I could have complained about the lack of a stunt coordinator, but I chose not to. The next scene was in the courtroom opposite my nemesis, Big Boy Caprice, who was played by Al Pacino. For the two days we worked together, he never spoke to me. At best, I got a nasty look. After a while, I got it. Al was a Method actor and always in his role. He was not supposed to like me, so he kept his distance. But the moment Warren said, *Cut,* he stuck out his hand and said, "Dick, how are you? How have you been?"

The whole experience baffled me. I never understood what I was doing there until finally, before leaving the set, I asked Warren why he wanted me.

"We needed somebody above reproach," he said. "We needed someone who was a good guy because of the twist at the end when he turns bad. I wanted someone nobody would ever suspect."

"And I'm the guy," I said.

"You're the guy." He nodded. "You're the goody two-shoes."

Hey, I guess it worked. The movie won three Academy Awards, Al Pacino received a Best Supporting Actor nomination, and the picture itself was a box-office smash. Michelle, who had known Warren for years, had the proper take. She advised me not to think too much about it, adding, "He and Madonna were fun to look at—and the movie was pretty good, too."

Perspective was one thing you hoped to acquire with age, and I suppose I was getting my share.

For my sixty-fifth birthday, Michelle threw me a party at

home. She put a big tent up in the backyard and took care of the
guest list without letting me in on who was coming. On the big
day, I walked in and saw a mob of people, seemingly everybody I
ever knew or had met, from all my leading ladies to Charlie Dye,
the kid who had lived next door to me when I was twelve and did
magic tricks with me. He had flown in from Indianapolis.

"You're not twelve anymore," I exclaimed.

"Neither are you," he laughed.

Beaming, Michelle watched us reconnect. She never explained how she had found him. The best part? Charlie had saved
an old magic trick of mine all these years, the endless-scarf trick,
and he gave it to me at the party. And I kept pulling and pulling . . . until both of us laughed the way we had fifty years earlier.

The party was sensational. We had a piano player. My daughter sang. Actually, all of us sang. I blew out the candles on my
cake and wanted to know how everyone else had gotten so old
when I was still a kid—or at least acted like one. I chalked it up
to good genes and a sense of humor.

Even my mother, at ninety-one, though having begun a marked
decline that eventually led to her death in 1993, still had a good
outlook. I had visited her over Mother's Day at Jerry's farm in
Arkansas, where he had moved after remarrying and she had soon
followed. We were on the porch, talking with one of my cousins,
and my mother turned to me and asked, "Who are these people?"
Her voice was so sweet and curious.

"That's your son Jerry," I said.

"Well, he looked like a nice man," she said. "I'm glad to
meet him."

She once called me in a panic. I heard the alarm in her voice
and started to look for my cell phone, thinking I should call my
brother while keeping her on the line. Then I heard the problem.

"You know your dad has left me," she said.

"Mom, . . ." I said.

"No, listen to me," she continued. "I fixed him breakfast and then he left. I thought he had gone to take a nap, but he's not in the bedroom." She paused. "Dick, I think he's run off with another woman."

Finally, it was my turn to speak.

"Mom, Dad has been dead for fifteen years," I said.

"Really?" she asked.

"Yes," I said.

"Oh, thank God!" she said.

H aving run nearly every television network on the planet— or at least seeming to have—Fred Silverman knew the TV business and also the business of TV. He was a throwback to the days when I started out and there were just a few guys in the executive suites who made all the decisions according to taste and gut instinct, as opposed to what the business had become now, with shows passing through a sieve of executives, committees, and focus groups before getting on the air.

I did not want to be seen as difficult, but I was spoiled by working with the best writers in the business, Carl Reiner, Aaron Ruben, Garry Marshall, Jerry Belson, Sam Denoff, and men of that ilk. As I told *People* magazine, it seemed to me that networks now pandered to an audience afflicted with "attention deficit disorders"—that is, if shows even made it through all the committees and testing—and so you needed someone with Fred's know-how to get a show on the air.

Like Warren Beatty, Fred also had a talent for hearing what he wanted to hear. Even when I refused his offer to star in a spin-off of his show *Jake and the Fat Man,* he kept right on talking as if I was going to change my mind, which eventually I did.

"I don't want to do an hour show," I said. "I think at my age— you know I recently turned sixty-five—it's going to be too much."

"Just do the pilot," he said.

"But that could turn into a commitment I don't want to make," I said.

"It could turn into an excellent series if we do our jobs," he said.

In 1991, I went on *Jake and the Fat Man* and introduced the character Dr. Mark Sloan, a free-spirited, iconoclastic physician who solves crimes in his spare time at night with his police detective son. Instead of picking up the pilot, CBS ordered three made-for-TV movies they called *Diagnosis Murder.* I made them contingent on casting my real-life son Barry as my TV son. The whole thing rode on that; otherwise I would not have agreed.

But they readily wrote him in and we went to work in Vancouver, planning to do the movies one after another. Cynthia Gibb and Stephen Caffrey were cast in the other key roles, and guest spots in the first movie went to Bill Bixby, Ken Kercheval, and Mariette Hartley. You could tell I had a say in developing my character. I had to play myself one way or another. I wanted him to be very human, very vulnerable—a little absentminded, caring, and funny when appropriate. Oh, and lest anyone miss all that, he danced.

For that first movie, I got Arthur Duncan, the great tap dancer from *The Lawrence Welk Show,* to come in and play a janitor. He secretly teaches me tap dancing in exchange for medical treatment. Nobody knows it, though. They keep hearing something going on in my office and wonder what it is. At the end of the show, we appear in the hall and do our number.

It was such a treat to dance with Arthur. I indulged myself. But while rehearsing, I did a move where I stepped on my heel and toe and all of a sudden my foot flopped. I could not step on my heel.

I called my doctor and he said get back here now if you don't want to lose the use of your leg. It was a pinched nerve, with some minor complications. We had to postpone the other two movies while I returned to L.A. and underwent several weeks of traction. By the time we finished the recast with Victoria Rowell and Scott Baio, there was talk about a series. And before long there was an order for eight episodes.

It was like the old Camel and the Arab fable: An Arab pitches a tent in the desert at night and leaves his camel outside. Complaining that he's cold, the camel asks if he can put his head inside. Then he asks if he can put his feet in. Before long, he's completely inside the tent. And so it was with *Diagnosis Murder* and me.

27

DIAGNOSIS FUN

O n a mild afternoon in February 1993, I stood facing a crowd on Hollywood Boulevard, feeling a mix of nostalgia and celebration. I was receiving a star on the city's Walk of Fame, the best part of which was sharing the moment with Michelle, who was at my side, as well as my former *Dick Van Dyke Show* costars Rose Marie and Morey Amsterdam, and the man responsible for the whole thing, Carl Reiner, who, when I turned to him and said thank you, quipped, "When I saw all of you here, I thought, Hey, we can do a show."

Given the chance, we might have. At any rate, we laughed and reminded ourselves of numerous good times from the old series. We reminisced about the production numbers we used to weave into some of the shows. Funny how all of us recalled those scenes as our fondest, especially Carl, who reminded us that they meant less writing and shorter scripts. But Morey was a musician,

Rosie was a singer, and of course Mary was a dancer, who back in the day continued to do her barre exercises at lunchtime. And all of us were hams.

As we stood on Hollywood Boulevard, I almost felt transported back in time as I remembered rehearsing a dance number with Mary that was set in a prison. Our legs were tied together, and as we practiced, I yanked her too hard and she fell. "Sorry, Mary," I muttered up into the sky now, hoping that wherever she was, she was able to hear me.

Oh, and then I remembered going to a recording studio with Mary after work one night to lay down vocals for a song, but the music had been prerecorded in the wrong tempo, way too fast, and we spent hours trying to get it right. It happened to be my fourteenth wedding anniversary that night and I never called home, sent flowers, or did anything. When I finally walked through the front door, my wife was waiting at the dining-room table for me, wearing a gorgeous evening gown, her candlelit dinner on the table, ruined.

Carl, Morey, and Rosie all felt my pain as I recounted that story thirty-some years later.

"I never knew that," Carl said.

"Boy, I was in deep trouble," I said.

"And so was your marriage," Morey said. "But things worked out. You still got your star."

My star was placed next to that of my idol, Stan Laurel, but when Hollywood's honorary mayor, Johnny Grant, finally unveiled it, there was an unexpected silence, followed by a clap of laughter. My name was misspelled. It read *Dick Vandyck*. Embarrassed, Johnny quickly handed me a Sharpie and I drew a line where there should have been a space and told him not to worry. It had happened before. When I opened in *Bye Bye Birdie,* the name on my dressing-room door was *Dyck Van Dyke*. I survived—and looking back, I learned not to sweat the little stuff.

Indeed, I rather enjoyed the reminder that even those immortalized are mortal, though there were those who were saying that I was looking more like TV's iron man. I was almost sixty-eight years old and had a show on CBS's fall schedule. Granted, it was Friday night at eight P.M., normally considered TV's dead zone, but I was content in trying to transform the graveyard into an old-age home, and who knows, maybe bring in some younger viewers, too.

It worked. Although the *Washington Post* described *Diagnosis Murder* as "prime-time television as it was twenty years ago," they were not criticizing me for that. On the contrary, they pointed out that there was an audience for *NYPD Blue* and one for my brand of entertainment, and added, "Buddy Ebsen didn't need to walk around bare-butted to make *Barnaby Jones* worth watching." I was pleased to find that viewers felt the same way. As a result, CBS ordered more shows beyond the initial eight.

For cost purposes, we'd shot the first round in Denver at a facility that had once been home base for the show *Ironside*. I stayed in Raymond Burr's former hotel penthouse, which had unobstructed views of the Mile High City. I could watch the sun rise and set from different sides of the glassed-in perch. I felt like I was suspended in the clouds, and I probably carried some of that lightness into the way I played this funny doctor who danced and roller-skated when he wasn't solving crimes.

It could not have been easier. But then, I feel as if every role is always a version of me.

The earliest version of me was put back on display on Nick at Nite, the bloc of nighttime programming the cable network devoted to classic shows. Some thirty years after its debut, *The*

Dick Van Dyke Show was a hit again. I don't mean this egotistically, but I was not surprised. However, others were. A reporter from the *Los Angeles Times* asked me why I thought the show was popular with a whole new generation, albeit a very different type of viewer from those who originally saw it.

The question made me laugh. Wasn't it obvious?

The show was funny.

It was the same reason kids still giggled through Laurel and Hardy movies. Some humor is timeless. Clever people like Carl Reiner come along and figure out new ways to find the funny in human behavior, and then all of a sudden you have another hit.

With two shows on the air, I supposed sticking to family entertainment all these years had paid off. I was hot.

And then I got too hot. At the start of November, as I was promoting both shows and an NBC Christmas special I'd narrated, Malibu was engulfed by wildfires. Michelle and I watched nervously as the flames danced slowly but steadily down the brush-covered hills. This happened every five or ten years; it was almost like payback for living amid such beauty close to the ocean.

Later that day, the sheriffs evacuated our neighborhood. There was no time to pack up the house, not even to gather more than a few photo albums. Michelle and I shut the door on all of our furniture and clothing, as well as a lifetime of possessions, artwork, and awards. We had no idea whether any of this stuff would be there when we returned—whenever that would be—or if it would even survive the rest of the afternoon.

Standing on the porch, I looked at her and shrugged. What were we going to do?

"We're leaving with each other," I said. "That's what's most important."

A short time later, I was updating my publicist, Bob Palmer,

when he put me on hold to talk to another client, Anthony Hop-
kins. A moment later, Bob came back on the phone and said that
Anthony, who also lived in Malibu, had called from London to get
the latest news on the fire. Hearing that Michelle and I were suddenly homeless, he offered us an apartment that he kept in West-
wood. Fortunately, we only had to spend one night there before
we were able to return to our house, which survived the close
call, as had all of the other homes in the neighborhood.

We were lucky. The flames had burned right into some of
the backyards. It was a lesson for all of us on how much you can
control in life, or rather, how little control you sometimes have.
As I'd found time and again throughout my life—and would
continue to find—you do what you can, say your prayers, and
hope for the best.

D efying predictions, we were renewed for a second season,
and production for *Diagnosis* moved to L.A., where we shot
at an old mental hospital off Coldwater Canyon Boulevard in the
Valley. The place was not haunted, but holes in the walls, urine
stains on the floor, and other damage made the torment of its
former occupants feel very close by. A moderate earthquake hit
one day and shook pieces of the ceiling loose. As they crashed to
the floor, it prompted jokes about the show's shaky status with the
network.

I turned seventy in the midst of the show's third season. I
joked that it was as hard to get out of the business as it was to
get in it. That season, Charlie Schlatter joined the cast in place
of Scott Baio. He added a personality that was like a missing
ingredient. I had spotted him when we were auditioning actors
to replace Scott. Fred Silverman had said, "I wish we could get a

Michael J. Fox type," and I said, "I've got just the guy. You couldn't get any closer to Michael J. Fox than Charlie Schlatter."

He fit in with Barry and me. The three of us would get all of our laughter out during rehearsal and then play the scenes as straight as possible. It was the same with Victoria. Off-camera, the three of us had a running joke. We used to wonder who was running the hospital while the three of us were out chasing a criminal or looking for clues. Luckily, I suppose, nobody ever asked.

I think the primary reason *Diagnosis Murder* succeeded was the relationship people saw on-screen between Barry and me. *That* was real. So was the bond I had with Charlie and Victoria. It was not your typical detective show. It felt more like Rob Petrie playing a detective. It may have looked that way, too, when we tossed in the roller-skating, singing and dancing, and wrapped it in a little cat-and-mouse mystery.

We lucked into something special, something you can't act, and when that happens, people will sense the fun you're having and tune in. They want to experience it, too.

We chugged along, the little TV show that could. When I looked up, we were in our sixth year. Then our seventh. In terms of longevity, the series surpassed *The Dick Van Dyke Show*. Astonished writers and TV insiders asked how that happened. *People* magazine called it "remarkable" that at nearly seventy-three years old I had a show. Was it remarkable?

Not to me. I just kept showing up and having fun.

I added to the fun by inviting many friends and contemporaries on as guest stars, including Mike Connors, Andy Griffith, Dick Martin, Sally Kellerman, Robert Vaughn, Tim Conway, and even Jack Klugman when he was recovering from throat cancer. I took pride in the easygoing, comfortable atmosphere. In fact, the only argument I ever had during the entire run came when the line producer tried to save money by cutting back on the sand-wiches we put out for the crew in mid-morning.

I heard grumbling right away. One thing you do not want on a TV series is an unhappy crew. I went straight to the producer and told him that if he was not going to pay for the sandwiches, I would out of my own pocket. Embarrassed, he had the food back the next day and smiles returned to my crew.

The only other problem I had came when the network brought on two young executive producers who tried to make the show hipper. All of a sudden a show opened with a guy in bed with a naked girl. And gun battles were written into the script. I told them that they were on the wrong show if they wanted to write cutting-edge stuff, and then I took my case to CBS presi-dent Leslie Moonves. Michelle had known Les many years earlier when he was a struggling actor, and that was probably why this powerful and astute man in TV who would have fit in nicely at the network back in its Tiffany heyday gave me ample time to air my complaint.

Indeed, Les listened as I told him that we did not need the sex and violence. I said that the people who tune in to the show did not expect it from me. Nor did they want it. Nor did I. In fact, I feared we would actually lose our audience if we kept it up.

Les heard me, and once that was straightened out, we chugged along for several more seasons. We finally wound down in 2001. By then we had spent ten years on the air.

But I did not go gently into the sunset. When we shot our finale, I invited a writer from the *Los Angeles Times* to come on the set for the purpose of giving him a piece of my mind about the poor treatment given us codgers by youth-obsessed TV and media outlets like the *Times,* who only seemed to care about the next big—and usually younger, sexier—thing. A few years earlier,

I had accused the *Times* of having "it in for us old folks" and sent one of their writers a letter that said, "Growing old is not a leper colony where an unfortunate few are sent to die. It is a precious gift given only to some lucky human beings."

At seventy-five, I thought I was ready to indulge in the gift of my dotage. I had been in the business for more than fifty years. "It's time to go out to pasture," I told the Associated Press. "Tastes have changed." I often felt like an anachronism because I stood for wholesome family entertainment, the stuff I had practiced and preached for half a century. But if that went out of fashion, well, what kind of society were we?

On the morning after our wrap party, where I had harmonized with the guys one last time, I stood on our front porch shaded in bougainvillea, draped my arm around Michelle, took a deep breath of ocean air, and for something like the fifty-seventh time in my career I announced my retirement.

Michelle laughed.

"How long do you think you'll be out in the pasture?" she asked.

I checked my watch and raised an eyebrow.

"What time is it now?"

Michelle was an excellent cook. She specialized in Italian food. The richer the sauce and the more garlic, the better. But for her, cooking was an artistic endeavor, and if she wasn't in the mood, we ate out. We also enjoyed a rich social life with Dolly and Dick Martin (they would always pretend to bicker, but it was an act and they were a wonderful couple), Tim Conway and his wife, Steve Lawrence and Eydie Gorme, Mike Connors and his wife, and Richard Crenna, who was a prince.

For a time, we also enjoyed poker night on Sundays at Barbara Sinatra's, though it was Michelle who played, not me. I kibitzed with Larry Gelbart, Jack Lemmon, and Veronique and Gregory Peck, who laughed at me when I said that I was the only one there who didn't play cards.

"Yeah," he said, "but you're the only one here still working."

That was true. After a few months of puttering around the house and checking the calendar to see which couple we were meeting for dinner, I told Michelle that I was going back to work. "I knew it," she chortled, her laugh echoing through the house. I made two *Diagnosis Murder* movies that aired on CBS in early 2002, one of which featured my daughter Stacy in a pivotal role, and the other included my grandson Shane, a budding actor and filmmaker whose energy and creativity made being on the set feel like the playground it had been for me forty years earlier.

After continuing to screw up my retirement with a guest spot on the NBC sitcom *Scrubs,* I reunited with Mary Tyler Moore for the first time since the sixties in a PBS production of *The Gin Game,* the Pulitzer Prize–winning play that Jessica Tandy and Hume Cronyn had made a Broadway hit in 1977. Before Mary and I had bid good-bye to the sitcom that made both of us household names, we'd said, "God, it would be fun to do a play together." Well, neither of us thought it would take nearly four decades.

The two-act play that brought us back together was about a couple of lonely people who meet at an old-age home and play gin rummy. Over the course of thirty-two games, their new friendship turns competitive, dark, and bitter—and in the end the two stubborn old mules miss the whole point of their second chance at companionship. Someone told me that Jessica and Hume had notes with dialogue hidden all over the stage, and I believed it.

Although Mary and I instantly recaptured our special chemistry, I could tell a couple days into the two weeks we set aside for rehearsal that we might have picked the wrong material. The director didn't give us much to work with, and I had problems with the coarse language. It never felt right calling Mary a bitch even though we were acting. We did a lot of takes and in the end it wasn't there, not the way I'd hoped.

Others disagreed. The play aired in May 2003 to mixed reviews, though it got a rave from actress Anne Bancroft. I bumped into her and her husband, Mel Brooks, one night at a restaurant shortly after the play aired and Anne was full of compliments and even a little envy.

"Why didn't you ask me to do it?" she said.

My jaw dropped.

"If you're telling the truth, I'm going to kill myself," I said.

As much as I enjoyed working again with Mary, I also would have loved to have worked with Anne.

Afterward, instead of rushing into more jobs, I tried behaving like an actual retiree for a change. An early riser, I worked out at the local gym, brought coffee to Michelle, and then disappeared for much of the rest of the day into the guesthouse, where I had a sophisticated computer setup to indulge my passion in computer animation and CGI. Few people realized it, but I had been the computer graphics specialist on *Diagnosis Murder*.

In my so-called retirement, I made short films, including some in 3D. I was like a mad scientist in his lab. I put my present-day self in an old *Dick Van Dyke Show* episode, and I cut and pasted myself into famous movies, which I then showed to my kids and grandkids, though their amusement hardly matched mine. I felt as if I had entered my second or third . . . make that my fifth or sixth childhood.

28

CURTAIN CALLS

I t was Carl's idea to do one more show. For years, we had resisted the idea of a *Dick Van Dyke Show* reunion. Although we understood the desire fans and network executives had to see all of us back together, it never appealed to most of us. Those things generally don't strike the right note with actors. Sure, fans get to take a nice, well-produced walk down memory lane and remember everything they loved about a show. They also get to see how everyone looks years later. But the actors don't want to be reminded of what they have lost or who looks more pickled than preserved.

We were a different bunch, too. We knew *The Dick Van Dyke Show* was really all about Carl Reiner. The show had started with him writing a full season of scripts and it had succeeded because of his genius as a writer. You can compare those shows with any great work of literature. It started and ended with the writing, and all of us knew it. That's why it ended after five special years. Carl wanted to move on. He was done with those characters. Like any ambitious writer, he had more he wanted to explore. And all of us knew that our roles in the show started and ended with his desire to continue breathing life into the characters he had created for us. We knew great TV began with great writing, not great acting, and that is a distinction that can't ever be ignored or underestimated. TV just won't work any other way. It all starts on the page.

And so when Carl stood onstage at the 2003 TV Land Awards and accepted that network's "Legend Award" by expressing his desire to do one more episode with the original cast, we paid attention. All of us heard about it immediately. Those who were not there in person received phone calls. Since reporters began contacting me almost as soon as he walked offstage, I got more details from Carl, who explained that he was going to write one more episode, the 159th as it were, bringing the characters up to date. He said he had an idea, and he sounded excited. That was enough for me.

"Count me in," I said.

Mary had the same reaction. So did Rosie. Sadly, the ensuing phone calls we made to one another and the rehearsals that followed reminded us of more than just the good times. We had lost some members of our TV family. Richard Deacon, who played Mel Cooley, had died in 1984. Two years later Jerry Paris, who had gone on to direct more than two hundred episodes of *Happy Days,* succumbed to a brain tumor that went undiagnosed until it was too late. He had called me from the hospital and was gone days later. Afterward, I wondered if the headaches he had always suffered from, as well as his sudden flare-ups of temper, were a result of the nascent tumor. Morey Amsterdam was our most recent loss. He died of a heart attack in 1996 at the age of eighty-seven. On the set, we spent a few minutes recalling some of his jokes, including a favorite—that he had moved into a Beverly Hills neighborhood so exclusive, the police had an unlisted phone number. We also missed Sheldon Leonard, who passed away in 1997.

The special, which aired in May 2004, hinged on Alan Brady hiring Rob and Sally for one last writing job, helping him prepare his funeral. He wanted a joke-filled eulogy written before he died. As for everyone's lives, Rob and Laura had moved into New York City, Ritchie was grown up (and bald), Sally had finally gotten married, and Millie was a widow who was dating my brother, Stacy (my brother, Jerry, reprised his role, too).

TV critics were kind and respectful, but most called it average and urged fans to revisit the original. I agreed with that assessment, too.

The show was just all right. But my attitude was this: If Carl, in his mid-eighties, wanted to tidy things up, I was going to help. At seventy-nine, I was still Rob Petrie, just like Mary was still the only one who fans wanted to hear say, "Oh, Rob!" As long as we were able to enjoy ourselves, we had to do it. Rosie said it was like a conversation we had picked up forty years later, and she was right. We had waited long enough.

All in all, I was glad we took the curtain call.

I liked to joke that I kept in shape to avoid assisted living, but I maintained a pace that would have had people half my age *hiring* an assistant. I made three detective movies for the Hallmark

Channel and then I put my limber limbs to work on *Night at the Museum,* an innovative family-oriented movie that came about when its star, Ben Stiller, and director, Shawn Levy, called and said they not only wanted me but *needed* me as well. I was beyond flattered—and ready.

In the movie, which starred Ben, Carla Gugino, and Robin Williams, I played a security guard trying to acquire the secret that enabled the museum's creatures to come to life. He was supposed to be the bad guy, but I played him as if he was misunderstood. Who wouldn't want eternal life? But after I did a dance scene, Ben began referring to me as "Dorian Van Dyke." The crew also joked that I must have found the secret to eternal youth when I insisted on doing all my own stunts—except for one that would have required me to fly on wires, stop myself against a wall, and drop down.

Having done that kind of stuff in *Mary Poppins,* I knew better. But by doing as much as I did, I surprised myself, and better still, I impressed the picture's young stuntmen, who cheered me on.

Awesome!

Would you look at that guy!

Did you see what that eighty-year-old dude just did?

They saw the part of me that only performers really understand. It was the part that came alive when the cameras were on and the director yelled, *Action.* Without a microphone, a camera, or a stage of some sort, without an audience to entertain, I withdrew into a place where I was more comfortable and recharged. I was aware that others saw me as private. On an *A&E Biography,* I was called a loner. People said that I was tough to know. If this was true—and I am not denying anything—it was not by design, not anything I did consciously. It's just that I have always been

like Stan Laurel and Buster Keaton—very shy and wary of expos-
ing too much of a sensitive gooey center, that is, until an opportunity arose to put a smile on someone's face.

Let me give you an example.

A few years earlier, I was sitting in my local Starbucks when
a young man came up to my table and introduced himself. In his
early thirties, Mike worked for director James Cameron, who had
an office nearby. He had seen me around, he said, and always
wanted to meet me. It turned out that he and a couple of other
guys regularly got together to harmonize and, knowing that I also
liked to sing, they wanted to know if I would join them sometime.
I had them up to the house that same night.

Their repertoire was mostly hip-hop, which I could not do,
so we tried some old barbershop things off sheet music I found
in my piano bench. From there we improvised, added tunes from
Mary Poppins, Chitty Chitty Bang Bang, and other Disney films,
and you know, it was the darnedest thing, but these three guys
and I sounded pretty good together—so good that we made our
get-togethers a habit. Soon we formalized our group as the Van-
tastix and sang at dinner parties and charity events.

My favorite venue, though, was the City of Hope, where we
went room to room, singing for kids battling cancer. In fifty-plus
years of show business, I never had a better audience. Most of
those little kids were bald, and a fair number of them could barely
sit up in bed, and there was a sad handful who could not even do
that. We stopped at the bed of a very sick fifteen-year-old boy. We
tiptoed into his room and quietly sang a song. He did not react.
Thinking he was asleep, we began to file out when suddenly we
heard a thin voice ask, "Could I hear another one please?"

We turned around and sang a whole bunch of songs. He

barely opened his eyes, but after we finished "Supercalifragilistic-expialidocious," I saw his mouth curl into a faint smile.

As far as I am concerned, applause does not get any louder.

In 1997, Margie was diagnosed with pancreatic cancer. A few years earlier, she had moved from the Oregon coast to Santa Fe, New Mexico. Both places shared a serenity that appealed to Margie and her taste for all things sparse and natural. She loved Santa Fe. But soon she was plagued by backaches. Despite treatment, they grew more debilitating and eventually she was diagnosed with cancer.

I arranged for her to get an apartment at the Motion Picture Home in Los Angeles. All the kids were here. It made sense.

Michelle and Margie never crossed paths, but they knew of each other almost as if they had met many times. Both were strong women. They shared a mutual respect.

We decorated Margie's place with new furniture and paintings, and she started intensive treatment. For a while, we thought she might pull through. But then she began to fail. At the end, she lapsed into a coma. For two weeks, the whole family sat beside her bed until she finally breathed her last breath. Quietly, I said good-bye and joined with the kids in crying, though I knew that in the end Margie was done suffering and had gone to a better place.

I was deeply affected. I had lost close friends like Richard Crenna, but Margie was the mother of my four children, someone who had been a part of my life practically since childhood, and even though we were long divorced, with her death I also lost a part of myself.

A year later, I was hit with more heartbreaking news.

Michelle's doctor found a spot on her lung and said he wanted to watch it. That was in January; by summer, it was determined that the spot was cancer. Michelle had surgery to remove the lower right lobe and we thought she was clean. But evidently she wasn't; a subsequent checkup showed that the cancer had metastasized. Though devastated, we vowed to fight on.

Everyone familiar with Michelle knew that she was a fighter to the core. She'd had three or four angioplasties since her first heart attack, and even though she was not as physically fit as she had been twenty years earlier, she still had the inner strength of an Olympic athlete. I took her to the hospital every day for chemo and radiation. It was not the most pleasant of routines, but we clung to statistics and prayer.

Sadly, though, Michelle did not respond to treatment. Several months before the end, her doctor gave me the news that we had tried our damnedest to avoid, and then deny: My beloved companion of nearly thirty-five years was not going to make it. As full of hope and fight as she was, Michelle was also scared. Every so often she broke down and asked me if she was going to die. I said that nobody knew but the doctors were doing their best— and they would not tell me if they did know. It was the hardest acting I have ever done.

As she neared the end, though, Michelle knew. It was October 2009, and she spent that time at home talking to her friends. She spent the last week of the month in a coma. Her doctor told me that she could still hear, so I sang and talked to her until the hospice nurses who were helping in the final days told me that she was gone.

I believe the last words she heard were "I love you."

I was completely unprepared for life without Michelle. I had read statistics showing that husbands rarely outlive their wives and I was prepared to leave her with a long to-do list, not the other way around. I mean Michelle was a world-class procrastinator. She postponed everything, including marrying me. You would think that the woman whose palimony suit made headlines for years would have insisted on cementing her future.

But no, not Michelle.

When she died, she left me a long list of unfinished projects. Like a bookshelf she wanted installed in the bedroom (it was three-quarters finished), a gazebo she planned to put on the hill in our backyard, and the wedding we had talked about for more than thirty years.

I'd wanted to get married at home, but when that seemed impossible to plan, I'd suggested a simple civil ceremony. I could still hear myself saying, "We don't have to tell anyone," and Michelle nodding, "Yes, that's a good idea, let's do it," and yet I could never get her to put a date on the calendar. The only thing she did not put off was her garden. She worked in the flower beds every day, and they were gorgeous all year round.

After she passed, I told the gardeners to keep them up the way she had, and they have been in constant bloom. Right now, on this warm day in mid-July, I am looking outside from the dining-room table and I see Michelle's garden full of vibrant color, full of life—just the way I remember her.

In the months that followed, I realized that I have not ever been without a companion looking out for me. There was my mother, then the Air Force, then Margie, and then Michelle. I found myself fumbling through the responsibilities of daily life, the little stuff they tell you not to worry about, which, I can tell you, is much easier to do when the closet is stocked with paper goods. On the bright side, only one of my credit cards was canceled before I got a system down for paying the bills.

Gradually, I found my footing. I turned into a hot commodity among the widows on the town's party circuit who needed a designated driver. In lieu of pot roast, I received invitations to all the charity events. But old age, as my friends will attest, is not a role I am ready to assume. I recently had dinner with Don Rickles and his wife and Mike Connors and his wife, all great friends who have evolved into a kind of super senior citizenship with good humor and all their marbles. If only the same could be said of their knees. When Don and Mike walked into the restaurant using canes, I cracked, "I have to hang out with a younger crowd!"

I was only half joking. Fortunately, though, the younger crowds still want to hang out with me. ABC's hit show *Dancing with the Stars* came calling, but I turned them down. As I told them, I can learn one dance, but a new one every week, and often two new dances, would be too strenuous. I sang and hoofed my way through a couple numbers with the L.A. cast of the *Mary Poppins* stage show. And I began work on a one-man show that is actually four men since it includes the three guys with whom I still harmonize every week.

In the nearly ten years since Mike first approached me at Starbucks, we have made two albums and sung at dozens of events, including one for hospital workers held in Anaheim. When I noticed that women in their sixties and up comprised most of the audience, I turned to the other guys in my group, all at least half my age, and warned them that these were my groupies.

Sure enough, after the show, the women rushed the stage, albeit slowly and politely. We had to make a run for it.

At the end of June 2010, we took the act to Washington, D.C.'s, Ford Theater and performed at a pre–July Fourth celebration for a crowd of dignitaries and politicians led by President Barack Obama and his wife, Michelle. At a reception beforehand, Michelle Obama gave me a great big hug and said, "Yours is my favorite television show of all time."

President Obama, standing next to her, chimed in, "She's not kidding. She won't miss it."

I asked if their daughters were going to attend the show.

"No, they have school tomorrow," Michelle said.

"But we're singing songs from *Mary Poppins*," I said.

"I'll make sure they see the tape," she said. "But they can't miss school."

The next night, our act went like gangbusters. When we sang "A Spoonful of Sugar," I threw in some special moves and noticed the president sliding down in his seat, laughing. Afterward, he came onstage and said, "You have to teach me some of those moves." He wanted to know how I still did it. Laughing, I said, "I don't have to get up in the morning and run the country."

O f all the presidents I have met (Johnson, Nixon, Clinton), Obama has been my favorite, though Bill Clinton was a lot of fun, too. Michelle and I met him when Carl was honored with the nation's Mark Twain Comedy Award in 2000. All of us got to chat with him in the Oval Office. We were ushered in two at a time. When Michelle and I walked in, I might as well have been invisible.

"At last we meet," he said to her, and that was it. The two of them spoke the whole time. I could have broken into a dance and they would not have noticed. Carl and his wife, Estelle, spent that night in the Lincoln Bedroom, and around midnight, shortly after they had gone to bed, there was a knock at the door. It was the president of the United States, wearing a sweatshirt and jeans. He sat down and talked to them until three A.M.

It was a very different side of the president, Carl told me. He was relaxed and even smarter than he appeared normally.

I had my public and private sides, too, but they are less different than I thought. The public saw a smiling, nimble-footed performer while my family and friends were served up a more contemplative loner, a man who many said was hard to know. Even my brother once said it was "difficult to get close" to me. I am not going to dispute any of that, though for the record I will say that it was not intentional. I was not even aware of it. But I have an explanation.

Throughout my whole life I have pondered the big questions. I've thought more like a philosopher or perhaps a minister, a career I briefly considered when I felt the calling as a teen. If I was hard to know, it was because I would disappear into this abyss of questions and debate. I would read the great thinkers and try to figure out what it all meant—my life and life in general. What was the point? What was I supposed to do? Was I getting it right?

I don't remember a time in my life when I wasn't asking those questions. But since losing Michelle and Margie, I've looked back on the years with a new perspective and considered the lessons I have learned as well as those that may have slipped past, and I've concluded that the answers I searched for were not that complicated, not nearly as much as they seemed. In fact, I may have known more than I gave myself credit for.

A few years ago, I told *Esquire* magazine that the Buddhists boiled it down to the essentials. They said you need three things in life: something to do, something to love, and something to hope for. The message does not get any clearer. I heard Walt Disney, Dr. Martin Luther King Jr., and Carl Reiner all say the same thing in their own way. Hope is life's essential nutrient, and love is what gives life meaning. I think you need somebody to love and take care of, and someone who loves you back. In that sense, I think the New Testament got it right. So did the Beatles. Without love, nothing has any meaning.

As corny as it sounds, I think my decision to stick with entertainment the whole family could see was made with that in mind. I am proud that I kept it clean, that I stood for something, and upheld values. I passed up a number of opportunities, but feel good about the contributions I have made, and the fan mail I receive is awfully nice, which is very satisfying. I wanted my work to reflect the kind of person I was—and wanted to be.

My mother said I was a good boy—and now, at almost eighty-five years old, in looking back, I guess I stayed that way. I simply did what I thought was right and got rid of most of my bad habits.

My best work was done at home. My kids turned out to be truly admirable people. Margie did the work, but I will take some credit. As the father of four, the grandfather of seven, and a great-grandfather four times over, why not? Best of all, I have noticed an improvement in each generation. I was a better father than my father, my sons have eclipsed me, and my grandchildren are on their way. Parenting in general has become more of a science, though I don't agree with everything I see these days—like the micromanaging of time. When I was young, when school let out for the summer, I used to have three months of barefoot time that was mine. I could do whatever I wanted. Now the kids don't seem to even have an hour by themselves to play and wax creative. What's going to be the effect of that?

As I've said many times, I've been lucky my whole life. I have worked with extraordinary people and always felt as if my work was play. I have also been fortunate that people have liked what I do, and as a result, they've liked me. I've tried never to take that for granted, to appreciate every compliment, kiss, and handshake, because I can imagine the opposite.

For nearly twenty years, I have volunteered at the Midnight Mission on L.A.'s skid row. Aside from fund-raising, I served food every holiday until I was asked to simply walk around as an unofficial maître d', which I interpreted as an invitation to sing with people, dance with some, or just sit at their table and have a conversation. One year, after I harmonized with a homeless woman, she said, "You don't know how many people look right through us, as if we're not even there."

I gave her a hug.

"I'm glad to be here," I said. "In fact, I can't think of anyplace else I'd rather be than right here, making you smile."

It is early morning, and I am at home. Come on in. Be careful not to trip over the ottoman. Just kidding. There isn't an ottoman or any other furniture blocking the path into the living room, where I have been augmenting the start of this beautiful day near the beach by playing jazzy chords on a black upright piano. It has not been tuned in thirty-some years, but all the keys work and it still sounds pretty darn good—just like me.

I said that the other day to a director who had come over to discuss working on my one-man play. He asked how the piano could still be in such good shape given the moist air, variations in temperature, and constant use. Good craftsmanship and luck, I said—the same reasons I'm still going strong today.

Over the past year, I have realized something about myself. I suffer from a form of claustrophobia: I hate being at home by myself. I am a people person. My life has been a magnificent indulgence. I've been able to do what I love and share it. Who would want to quit? I suppose that I never completely gave up my childhood idea of being a minister. Only the medium and the message changed. I have still endeavored to touch people's souls, to raise their spirits and put smiles on their faces.

It seems that I have done a good job. But the awards I have received over the years pale in comparison to the memories I've collected. I began talking about retirement fifty years ago. What the hell was I thinking? What was going on in my head? I can't imagine what I would have done. These days I no longer talk about stopping or even slowing down. I am happily, contentedly resigned to the fact that that won't happen, not as long as I have a say in the matter.

As you may have guessed, there is no end to this story—not yet, anyway. So instead of a tidy conclusion, I will let you in on my plans. Right now I am going to take my wirehaired terrier, Rocky (he wanted to see his name in the book), for a walk. Later I have rehearsals at an L.A.-area high school where I perform with the kids each year at a fund-raiser. They seem to like it, but not half as much as I do. Coming up are meetings for my one-man show. And then, who knows.

As always, I will see where the wind takes me.

ACKNOWLEDGMENTS

A life story consists not of one life but of many, and after reading the last draft of this book I realized how many dear and precious friends have contributed to the richness of my life. I'm afraid it would take a stack of books five feet tall to thank everyone. But I do want to mention a few key people without whom my life would not have been as lucky. They include Phil Erickson, Byron Paul, Carl Reiner, Walt Disney, Aaron Ruben, Sol Leon, Marc Breaux and Dee Dee Wood, Danny Daniels, Chita Rivera, Mary Tyler Moore, Gower Champion, Mary Miller, Pansy Legg, and my incredible family—children and grandchildren. Special thanks must also go to my editor, John Glusman, as well as to the entire Crown team, especially Domenica Alioto, Tina Constable, Mark McCauslin, Barbara Sturman, Jennifer O'Connor, Court Clinch, and Shaye Areheart. And finally a thanks to my team on this project: my book agent, Dan Strone; my manager, Jeff Kolodny; my publicist, Bob Palmer; and my collaborator, Todd Gold.

INSERT PHOTOGRAPH CREDITS

Page 4, above: Photofest

Page 5, above: CBS/Photofest; below: Photofest

Page 7, above: Walt Disney Productions; below: Walt Disney Productions/Photofest

Page 8, above and below: Walt Disney Productions/Photofest

Page 11, above: United Press International; below: United Artists/Photofest

Page 13, above: NBC/Photofest

All other photographs are from the author's collection.

INDEX

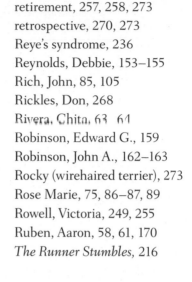

8/19/11